# Production Activity Control

## A Practical Guide

# Production Activity Control

## A Practical Guide

**Steven A. Melnyk,** Ph.D., CFPIM
**Phillip L. Carter,** Ph.D., CFPIM

*Both of the*
*Department of Management*
*Graduate School of Business Administration*
*Michigan State University*

*With contributions from:*

**Walter R. Gartman**
Corporate Director, CLAMPS/BRP
*The Vollrath Corporation*
*Sheboygan, Wisconsin*

**Michael Hablewitz,** CPIM
Vice President, Materials Management
*Twin Disc Incorporated*
*Racine, Wisconsin*

**William R. Wassweiler,** CPIM
*MRM, Incorporated*
*Brookfield, Wisconsin*

**John Treffert,** CPIM
*MRM Associates*
*Brookfield, Wisconsin*

**Ronald Pannesi,** CPIM
*University of North Carolina*
*Chapel Hill, North Carolina*

DOW JONES-IRWIN
Homewood, Illinois 60430

658.5

ISBN 0-87094-970-5

Library of Congress Catalog Card No. 86–72273

*Printed in the United States of America*

1 2 3 4 5 6 7 8 9 0 K 4 3 2 1 0 9 8 7

In any well-run manufacturing system, two ingredients are always present: good plans complemented by good control over the execution of these plans. This book focuses on *production activity control* (PAC), the component of the manufacturing planning system that is directly responsible for controlling the execution process on the shop floor. It identifies and discusses the principles and practices of effective production activity control.

Production activity control (PAC) is the set of activities required to convert the orders released by the manufacturing planning system to the shop floor into completed orders. Although every manufacturing firm, irrespective of size, product made, and location, must have a PAC system, few firms now have *effective* PAC systems. Few firms are now able to consistently deliver a quality product a the time, price, and place promised. For many firms, the shop floor is not under control; it is out of control. Although many firms are able to formulate good plans, few are able to implement these plans successfully on the shop floor. In most firms, the PAC system is informal and poorly controlled by management.

In large part, what makes effective PAC difficult to achieve is that it is not well understood. Most manufacturing managers are able to identify some of the individual activities of PAC (e.g., dispatching, data collection), but few have been able to grasp the concept of PAC as a *total system*. Production activity control is not the same as the shop floor reporting system, nor is it the same as the dispatching system. These activities are only elements within the total PAC system.

For many managers, PAC is the source of much confusion as well as frustration. This book is intended to remove that confusion by identifying, summarizing, and examining the principles and practices of *effective* production activity control. Specifically, the book:

1. Identifies what production activity control is.
2. Discusses the major activities of a production activity control system.
3. Identifies the prerequisites to effective PAC.
4. Examines the implementation and execution of the various activities of PAC.
5. Identifies how to effectively interface the PAC system with other groups in the firm, including engineering, quality assurance, finance, and marketing.

By the end of the book, the reader should:

- Be aware of what production activity control is.
- Be aware of the importance of an effective PAC system to both the manufacturing planning system and the firm as a whole.
- Be aware of the costs incurred and the benefits obtained from the implementation and use of an effective PAC system.
- Recognize the linkages that exist between PAC and such functional areas of the firm as cost accounting, quality control, manufacturing engineering, engineering, and maintenance.
- Be acquainted with the minimum requirements that must be in place before an effective PAC system can be implemented.
- Be familiar with the five major activities that are normally considered essential components of PAC:
  Order review/release.
  Detailed scheduling.
  Data collection/monitoring.
  Control/feedback.
  Order disposition.
- Be aware of and appreciate the key role played by an effective capacity planning system and shop floor personnel in the successful operation of the PAC system.
- Recognize that how the PAC activities are carried out varies by the type of manufacturing environment (i.e.,

project, job shop, repetitive/continuous), the type of production (i.e., make-to-stock, make-to-order, engineer-to-order, and assemble-to-order), and the size of the firm.
- Be aware of the extent to which the computer can be used to enhance the operation of an effective PAC system.
- Recognize the differences in the methods for scheduling and controlling:
   Preventive maintenance.
   Salvage.
   Scrap.
   Rework.
- Be aware of the "dos and don'ts" of effective production activity control.
- Be familiar with the major steps in the successful implementation of an effective PAC system.
- Recognize the characteristics of an effective PAC system.
- Be familiar with the terminology of production activity control.

For many managers, PAC has become the shoal on which well-formulated plans flounder. It does not have to be so. Once the basics of PAC are understood, an effective PAC system can be built. This book identifies and discusses these basics. An effective PAC system can enable the firm to successfully manage and control costs and lead times—two important dimensions on which most firms compete. Effective PAC offers managements a method of differentiating themselves from their competition in an increasingly competitive marketplace.

## ACKNOWLEDGMENTS

In addition to the contributors listed on the title page of this book, the authors would like to thank the following individuals for their help on it:

   Jim Austhof, Production and Inventory Control, Chair Plant, Steelcase, Inc., Grand Rapids, Michigan
   Jack E. Durben, Consumer Healthcare Division, Miles Laboratories, Elkhart, Indiana
   David M. Lyth, Assistant Professor, University of Wisconsin—Eau Claire, Wisconsin.

These people provided helpful suggestions on how the book should be structured. They were instrumental in identifying the directions to be taken and in providing examples to help illustrate the points made.

As with any book, any errors and omissions remain the sole responsibility of the authors.

**Steven A. Melnyk**
**Phillip L. Carter**

# CONTENTS

# CHAPTER ONE

# Production Activity Control: A Framework

Production activity control—also called job shop control [2], manufacturing activity planning (MAP) [6], and shop floor control (SFC) [11][1]—is a vital element of any successful manufacturing system. Before the reader can appreciate the importance of PAC, the term *production activity control* must be defined. This book employs a broad definition:[2]

> [Production activity control] is that group of activities directly responsible for managing the transformation of planned orders into a set of outputs. It governs the *very short-term* detailed planning, execution, and monitoring activities needed to control the flow of an order from the moment the order is released by the planning system for execution until the order is filled and its disposition completed. The [production activity control] system is responsible for making the detailed and final allocation of labor, machine capacity, tooling, and materials to the various competing orders. It collects data on the activities taking place on the shop floor involving the progress of various orders and the status of resources and makes this information available to the planning system. Finally, the [production activity control] system is responsible for ensuring that the shop orders released to the shop floor by the planning system are completed in a timely and cost-effective manner.

---

[1]The references identified by the numbers in brackets are listed on pages 157–58.

[2]This definition is based on the shop floor control definition offered in [11, p. 35].

**FIGURE 1** Major Components of the Manufacturing System

Corporate planning system

**Upstream systems**

Production planning

Formal manufacturing planning system

Master scheduling

Material planning ← → Capacity planning

Provide the downstream systems with:

* Resources
* Production objectives
* Priorities
* Overall direction

Provide the upstream systems with:
* Output
* Manufacturing capabilities
* Feedback on products, costs, standards

Production activity control

**Downstream systems**

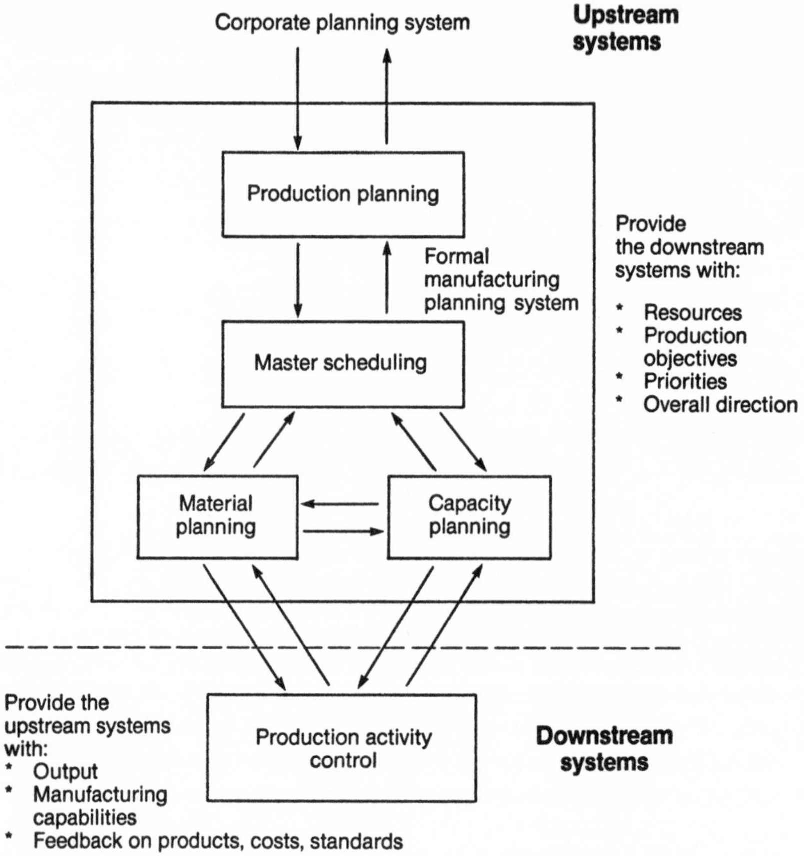

This definition views production activity control as a subsystem within the entire manufacturing system. That is, production activity control complements such other planning systems as material requirements planning and capacity requirements planning. These other systems, the "upstream" systems of Orlicky [13, pp. 46–47], provide the resources required by the PAC system and set the objectives of that system. Production activity control, a "downstream" system, is then responsible for using the resources provided to achieve those objectives in an effective and efficient fashion. The relationship between the planning system and production activity control is summarized in Figure 1.

## THE SHOP ORDER

A focal point of any PAC system is the *shop order.* All the activities of the PAC system are directed at ensuring the timely and efficient completion of shop orders.

Simply defined, a shop order is a planning system *authorization* for the shop floor to produce a predetermined quantity of a particular item (identified by its part number) that is to arrive into inventory at a specified time (typically referred to as the "order due date"). The authorization may be a piece of paper produced by the planning system (a "hard copy") or a message found in the manufacturing data base (a "paperless" release). In either case, the shop order allows the PAC personnel to allocate shop floor resources (material inventory, machine capacity, labor, and tooling) against the order. The generation of the shop order marks the starting point for the PAC system.

The form of the shop order is dependent on the specific manufacturing environment in which the PAC system is found. There are two major categories of manufacturing settings:

Repetitive/continuous manufacturing.
Discrete batch (job shop) manufacturing.

Generally speaking, repetitive/continuous manufacturing is concerned with the production of high-volume standard items. These items are produced either in discrete units (e.g., box wrenches, appliances, automobiles) or in continuous flow (e.g., fluids, power, petroleum). In both cases, the shop orders to be released to the floor for a given day are aggregated into a daily run schedule. This schedule, not the individual shop orders, is used to authorize and control production.

Job shop manufacturing is characterized by extreme variability in product design, process requirements, and order quantities. In general, such manufacturing deals with a large number of relatively small shop orders. In this setting, the PAC system must deal with *individual* shop orders. The daily run schedules of repetitive/continuous manufacturing are not feasible.

The PAC system must manage two flows accompanying the shop order. The first flow is the product flow and the attendant physical allocation of resources. The second flow is the information flow. As the shop order moves through the various stages of processing, information is generated that personnel both inside and

**FIGURE 2** Flows between the PAC and the Planning Systems

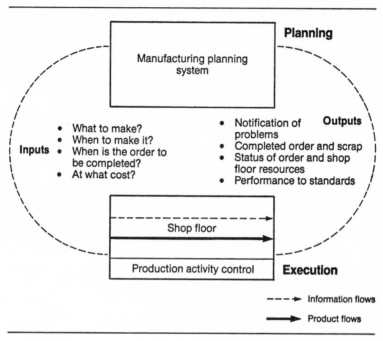

outside the PAC system use in monitoring the progress of the order. This information closes the loop between the planning and execution components of the manufacturing system (see Figure 2).

## FORMS OF THE SHOP ORDER

When first released by the planning system, the shop order is simply a "statement of intent." It describes the requirements of the planning system in terms of such attributes as quantity, part number, and *order* due date. As the order moves from operation to operation on the shop floor, it undergoes a series of physical changes. At each operation, the addition of material components, labor, tooling, and machining alters the order, bringing it ever closer to the desired finished form. After each operation has been completed, a decision must be made about how next to handle the order. This decision is based on a comparison of the actual quality progress of the order with its planned progress.

If the actual quality progress of the order (when compared to its planned progress) is within tolerance limits acceptable to management, the order is directed to the next operation (as specified in its routings). However, if the actual quality progress is unacceptable, management must initiate some form of corrective action. In some cases, simply rescheduling the problem order may correct the problem. In most cases, however, correcting the problem requires management to change the order, *either in whole or in part,* into one of three other forms: rework, salvage, or scrap. Each form requires different handling by the PAC system.

## Rework

Rework is the portion of a shop order that requires extra processing or special handling. The most frequent reason for rework is to correct processing problems. That is, not all of the parts processed through a given operation meet quality specifications. Some parts may be unacceptable due to *correctable* processing defects (e.g., excessive or insufficient cutting, insufficient grinding). These parts can be made acceptable by adding labor, material, or processing. As a result, rework often requires a change in the standard routing to reflect these corrective actions. The lead time for rework items is usually longer than that of "normal" or no-rework items. When the corrective actions have been *successfully* completed, the rework portion of the order should meet the quality specifications.

Since rework items require different handling, many manufacturing systems give them their own identity. That is, the rest of the original order is adjusted to reflect the effect of rework (the order quantity is reduced by the amount of rework) and a new order, with its own due date and order quantity (equal to the amount of the rework), is created. The new order due date may or may not be the same as the order due date of the original order (depending on the amount of additional lead time needed for rework). The two orders are controlled separately by the planning system. The operator at the next stage of the routing is not held responsible for the rework quantity; he is held responsible only for the quantity that he receives. By creating new order identities for rework items, we recognize that rework cannot be controlled in the same way as nonrework. This maintains the integrity of the system.

Rework is a *temporary* form for a shop order. If the rework can be corrected to meet current quality standards, the reworked parts disappear as a separate entity as soon as they have completed the rest of the route. However, if the rework cannot be completed as required, it undergoes a further transformation—into either "salvage" or "scrap."

## Salvage

Salvage describes the portion of a shop order that cannot be completed as initially planned and released. Although the items in that portion cannot be recovered by converting them into a rework order, they can still be useful to the system in one of two forms: order salvage or component salvage.

In order salvage, the affected items can be processed and completed into different finished items—items that the planning system did not plan for but that it can still use. A classic example of salvage is the conversion of a 60-inch bolt of cloth into a 48-inch bolt. The cloth can no longer be completed as a 60-inch bolt because of a material defect in the outer 12 inches. Thus, the order can no longer be completed as initially released. The planning system, however, can use a 48-inch bolt of cloth. As a result, the defective bolt can be saved by recutting it into a 48-inch bolt.

Component salvage, in contrast, involves recovering any components used in the manufacture of the affected items. For example, a computer board assigned to salvage contains several expensive chips. During salvage operations, a worker removes these chips and returns them to component stores (where they increase the on-hand balance).

When dealing with salvage, management is often faced by two decisions: which form of salvage to use and when to complete the salvage operations. In many instances, a salvage item can be either completed (as a different item) or it can be broken down and its components salvaged. Management must decide which form of salvage is most useful to the manufacturing system at the given time. Second, since the items produced by salvage are not needed by the planning system at that time, management must decide when to complete them. Often the completion of salvage operations is triggered by the availability of excess capacity on the shop floor.

Like rework, salvage must be treated as a separate entity by the planning system.

Salvage can generate two different effects. First, if completed, it can result in an unplanned increase in inventory (at either the component level or the completed assembly level). The planning system may then have to adjust its production schedule to reflect this "unanticipated" change in inventory. Second, if all or part of a shop order becomes salvage, then the order, as initially planned and released, can no longer be completed. The quantity of the original order is now decreased by the amount of salvage, and the planning system now has an unfilled need. Consequently, the presence of salvage may require the release of another shop order that is primarily "remedial" (i.e., intended to fulfill the initial needs of the planning system).

## Scrap

Scrap denotes an order that can no longer be completed into a part usable by the system either as originally intended or as salvage. For all purposes, scrap is useless to the planning system. This does not mean that scrap is completely useless. Scrap often has high value when it is sold to an outside processor. In the case of scrap, the PAC system must still account for the shop order and must supervise its disposal.

Scrap should never be confused with salvage. Unlike salvage, which results in items or components that are still usable by the planning system, scrap is not usable by the system. A defective part that can be remelted into a metal ingot is salvage; a defective part that the system must throw out is scrap.

The PAC system must recognize that as any shop order progresses through the various operations on the shop floor, it can take on several different forms. The form taken can change from operation to operation. The PAC system must be able to control the movement of the shop order irrespective of the form it takes.

## MAJOR RESOURCES CONTROLLED BY
## THE PAC SYSTEM

The PAC system manages the transformation of a shop order from the planned state to the completed state by allocating various quantities of four primary resources to the order. These resources are:

- *Personnel.* All of the personnel that the PAC system can draw on in executing the plans released to it. This resource includes overtime, workers transferred from other locations, part-time help, and multiple-shift operations. It also includes both direct and indirect labor.
- *Tooling.* All of the equipment and special fixtures that the PAC system can draw on and use during the setup and operation of a machine or an assembly process.
- *Machine Capacity.* The total amount of productive capacity offered by the equipment available.
- *Material.* The total stock of the components used in completing the shop order.

In addition to these primary resources, the PAC system can control such other resources as special handling equipment. Of these four resources, the first three define the major elements of capacity for the PAC system.

The PAC system and its personnel are held responsible for how these various resources are used. Thus, the PAC system can be evaluated on its ability to efficiently manage these resources (as measured in terms of the tooling, material, machine, or labor variances). The PAC system is not responsible for determining the level of each resource. That task is a responsibility of the planning system *alone.*

The planning system determines the total amount of material available. It also determines the number of labor-hours that will be available in any one period. In this sense, the planning system "constrains" the PAC system by placing upper limits on resource availability—upper limits that the PAC system can never exceed. The PAC system is then responsible for working within these limits. It makes the detailed allocation of resources to the various shop orders and monitors the use of these resources.

# MAJOR ACTIVITIES OF PRODUCTION ACTIVITY CONTROL

Production activity control governs five major groups of activities:

Order review/release
Detailed scheduling
Data collection/monitoring
Control/feedback
Order disposition

These five groups encompass the entire process of transforming a planned order into a completed order. A schematic of that process and of the positioning of these five groups is provided in Figure 3.

## Order Review/Release

Order review/release consists of the activities that must be completed before an order can be released to the shop floor. These activities are necessary to ensure that the orders released have a *good* chance of being completed by the time required. Order review/release consists of four activities, the first of which is order documentation.

**Order Documentation.** An order is simply a planning system authorization for the shop floor to begin production. The amount of information needed by the planning system in creating and releasing an order is far less than the amount needed by the shop floor. Order documentation provides information needed by the shop floor but not provided by the planning system when an order is released. Typically, the following information is added to an order by this activity:

- *Order Identification.* A number or code assigned to an order before it is released to the shop floor. This number can be used to track the order once it is on the shop floor and to retrieve information about the order (e.g., processing time or next operation). The order identification number (which should be distinct from the part number) links

**FIGURE 3** PAC: An Integrative Framework

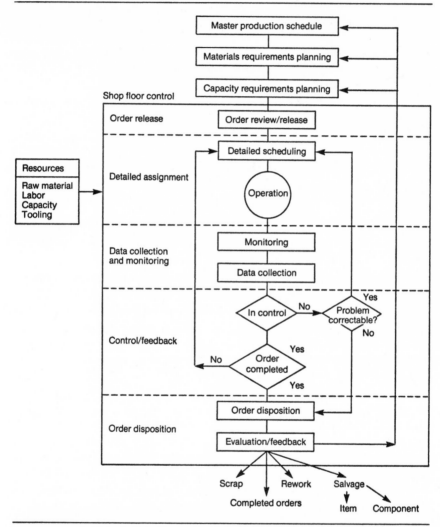

SOURCE: S. Melnyk, P. L. Carter, D. M. Dilts, and D. M. Lyth, *Shop Floor Control* (Homewood, Ill.: Dow Jones-Irwin, 1985), p. 40.

the shop floor to the planning system. Depending on the system, the assignment of the order identification number can be done either by the planning system on release of the order to PAC or by the PAC system.

• *Routings.* The various operations (and their sequence)

through which an order must pass. Routings help identify the order's resource requirements.

- *Time Standards.* The resources (machine and labor) and the amount of time that each resource should *reasonably* require at each stage in the shop floor transformation. This information is essential for order sequencing (dispatching), monitoring, and capacity management.
- *Material Requirements.* The raw materials and components (described in terms of specific part numbers and quantities) needed by an order and the specific stage in the processing at which these components are needed.
- *Tooling Requirements.* The tooling required, the time that it should require, and the stage in processing at which it is required must be identified at this stage in PAC, and this information must be added to the shop order. The information in question forms the basis for issuing the tooling order and for planning tooling requirements.
- *Other.* Other information provided at this stage may include specific report forms, operation due dates, anticipated scrap levels, and any special handling requirements.

The information required by order documentation can be taken from a set of files that are either centrally located (in the form of a common data base) or dispersed in the various departments of the firm. In the latter case, the information on routings and time standards, for example, might be found in the engineering files. PAC requires the presence of an up-to-date, accurate, and complete manufacturing data base. This requirement (a prerequisite of any effective PAC system) is discussed in detail later in this book.

**Material Checking.** Another major order review/release activity is checking the inventory status of the components and raw materials required by the shop order to ensure that they will be available in sufficient quantity at the necessary time and place. As a rule, shop orders should never be released to the floor in the face of insufficient component inventory. By ensuring that all orders released will have the necessary components, the PAC system keeps work-in-process low and avoids needlessly tying up shop capacity.

Material availability need not be checked before releasing the order if the formal material planning system is working effectively and shop floor personnel have confidence that this system can deliver the necessary parts.

**Capacity Evaluation.** Inventory availability, while important, is not enough. There must be adequate capacity available for the order. In the capacity evaluation stage of order review/release, the capacity required by the shop order is compared with the capacity available in the system. At this stage, a judgment must be made as to whether the available capacity is adequate. If not, the release of the order may be delayed until the necessary capacity becomes available. Evaluating and controlling capacity loading on the shop floor avoid shop overloading and the resulting increasing queues and lengthening lead times.

**Load Leveling.** In many PAC systems, the orders that are recommended for release by the planning system are not always released immediately. Instead, they are often accumulated (backlogged) for a short period of time and released to the floor at a controlled rate in order to *level* the resulting shop load. The objective of this load leveling activity is to level capacity utilization by smoothing out the peaks and valleys of the load on work centers. The pool of backlogged orders effectively decouples the planning system from the shop floor.

The various activities of order review/release are basically short-term planning activities. They do not require that the resources required by the various orders actually be committed. Instead, they are primarily concerned with determining whether the current level of resources is sufficient to justify the release of the orders to the shop floor. The actual commitment of resources is the major focus of the second set of PAC activities—detailed scheduling.

## Detailed Scheduling

One of the most visible activities associated with any PAC system involves the determination and assignment of operation priorities to orders that await processing. These activities are part of the second major activity of PAC—*detailed scheduling.*

Detailed scheduling (or detailed assignment) describes the process by which personnel from the PAC system manage the detailed allocation of the major shop floor resources (people, machines, tooling, and material). These resources must be used not only to complete the shop orders currently on the floor but also to conduct the "nonproductive" activities necessary to ensure the continued availability of these resources (e.g., *scheduled* preventive maintenance).

When matching shop floor resources with the demands placed on them, the assignment decisions must be very detailed. These decisions should address the following concerns:

1. *Types of Resources.* The assignment should identify the specific types of resources to be used.
2. *Quantities of Resources.* The assignment should identify the amounts of the resources to be used (e.g., the amount of labor to be assigned to a specific order may be identified in terms of the standard labor-hours).
3. *Timing of Assignment.* The assignment should identify in clear terms the time at which the resources are to be assigned, the time over which the assigned resources are to be used, and the expected time at which the resources are to become available for reassignment.
4. *Placement of Resources.* If the resources to be assigned can be obtained from more than one location, the assignment should identify the specific locations from which the necessary resources are to be obtained.
5. *Priority of Processing.* Finally, the assignment should identify the sequence in which the competing demands are to be permitted access to the resources. These priorities are often identified by means of a dispatching rule.[3]

Detailed scheduling embodies three major activities: (1) order sequencing/dispatching, (2) scheduled maintenance, and (3) other assignments.

**Order Sequencing/Dispatching.** Order sequencing/dispatching deals with the most visible of the detailed scheduling activities—

---

[3]This aspect of assignment decisions is discussed in greater detail later in Chapter Five.

the assignment of resources to the various competing orders. In this book, order sequencing/dispatching is defined as

> the process of determining by means of a prespecified set of decision-rules the sequence in which a facility is to process a number of different shop orders. When processing these orders, order sequencing/dispatching is also responsible for the corresponding assignment of workers, tooling, and material to the selected jobs. The sequencing of resource assignment is consistent with a predetermined set of goals that the [production activity control] system attempts to satisfy (i.e., meeting order due dates, reducing maximum lateness of orders, etc.). [11, p. 44]

In many production systems, operation priorities are determined by means of a decision rule that is commonly referred to as a "dispatching rule" or a "priority rule." The resulting priorities are communicated to people on the shop floor by means of the "dispatch list." This list, which is usually produced daily, displays all of the shop orders waiting in queue at a given work center in a priority sequence derived from the dispatching rule being used. The dispatch list is a major input into the order sequencing/dispatching process.

**Scheduled Maintenance.** Scheduled maintenance, the second activity of the detailed scheduling phase, involves the assignment of resources to preventive maintenance. Lubrication, inspection, and periodic overhauls of machinery are examples of scheduled maintenance.

All PAC systems need scheduled maintenance because the resources used are subject to the wear and tear that day-to-day operations place on them. Machines break down periodically, and when they do, the production capabilities that they offer are temporarily lost. One rule with which most shop floor personnel are familiar is that machines always break down when they are needed most.

The longer resources are operated without scheduled maintenance, the greater is their chance of experiencing a breakdown. The intent of scheduled maintenance is to reduce the risk of machine breakdowns. Scheduled maintenance is considered part of the detailed scheduling phase because preventive maintenance activities often compete with shop orders for access to machines.

**Other Assignments.**   Shop resources can be assigned to other activities such as scheduled downtime or indirect labor. Such activities are intended to level current capacity utilization (scheduled downtime) or to utilize currently available shop floor resources that are not required by orders for other tasks (e.g., the transfer of workers to indirect labor activities).

The assignment of capacity to scheduled downtime is becoming more important as a result of the increased use of just-in-time principles and practices. Inventory buildup frequently occurs between two machines or work centers with different output rates. One method of preventing such buildup is to periodically schedule downtime for the higher-output work center. In this way, scheduled downtime provides management with one method of balancing output.

## Data Collection/Monitoring

Information is crucial in any PAC system, for it is the major linkage between the planning system and the shop floor. The flow of this information is bidirectional. The planning system keeps the shop floor informed of any changes in the planned requirements (e.g., the cancellation/addition of orders; customer-requested changes in order due dates); the PAC system keeps the planning system aware of the progress of all open orders. Such information is collected and analyzed by the data collection/monitoring activity of the PAC system.

Data collection records information from the shop floor. Information typically collected includes:

Current location of shop orders.
Current state of completion of orders.
Actual resources used at the various operations.
Actual resources used at preceding operations.
Unplanned delays encountered.

Such information is often collected in terms of physical units and costs. While physical units are meaningful to the people floor, the progress of the shop floor is often more easily understood by others in the firm if it is stated in terms of *costs*.

Once the information has been collected, it must be analyzed (i.e., monitored). This analysis is frequently done by comparing the actual progress of a job with its planned progress. The progress of a shop order can be measured along several different dimensions: stage of completion, costs incurred to date, amount of scrap produced, or nearness to due date. Progress must be compared with standards taken from engineering or accounting information, past performance (e.g., last month's performance), or management's expectations. Ultimately, the purpose of monitoring is to identify those orders that, by virtue of the large discrepancy between actual and desired levels, require special management attention.

### Control/Feedback

There is a point at which actual performance is viewed as being unacceptable to management. This point must be determined by management before the order is released to the PAC system; it must be known to the people working on the shop floor. The margin of error should reflect such considerations as the relative costs of having late and early orders. Whenever performance becomes unacceptable, the PAC personnel must step in. They can take two forms of corrective action: control and feedback.

**Control.** In the short term, adjustments can be made in shop floor capacity. Examples of such adjustments include:

Changes in the work rate.
Use of overtime or part-time labor.
Use of safety capacity.
Alternative routings.
Lot splitting.
Subcontracting of excess work.

These adjustments are intended to bring the actual progress of shop orders within an acceptable distance of the desired progress.

**Feedback.** Information pertaining to the progress of orders on the shop floor is transmitted from the PAC system to the planning system. This information linkage keeps the planning system aware of what is happening on the shop floor; it also identifies for the planning system those orders for which the capacity adjustments of the PAC system are insufficient.

At this stage, the planning system may intervene to correct the problem. It may take the following remedial actions:

The need date for the order may be changed.
The order may be canceled.
The incoming load may be reduced.
The order quantity may be reduced.

These actions alter the demands that the planning system places on the PAC system. As a rule, they should be taken only *after* the PAC system has exhausted the control options available to it.

Important in control/feedback is the creation and use of *exception reporting*. At this stage in the PAC system, information that requires management action is available. Exception reporting directs this information to the responsible managers. The managers who most need the information are given first access to it.

## Order Disposition

The last stage of PAC is order disposition. Order disposition includes *all* of the activities required to transfer orders out of the PAC system. This stage is responsible for both completed orders and scrap. Order disposition has two major objectives: (1) to relieve the shop floor of responsibility for the orders and (2) to provide the rest of the firm with ending information on which to evaluate the performance of the shop floor.

At the completion of order disposition, the PAC system is no longer responsible for the items. These items can be disposed of in two ways. In the case of acceptable completed items, they can become part of the firm's inventory stocks. Such items are now treated as assets by the accounting system. In the case of scrap, the items can be disposed of to one or more "profit and loss" accounts. If there is no recoverable salvage value, the cost of the scrapped items is charged off to an expense account (e.g., Scrap Expenses). If there is some recoverable salvage value, the scrapped items can be charged off to a combination of revenue and expense accounts. Irrespective of how an order is treated, the point to be noted here is that it must be accounted for in terms of both unit quantities and cost.

At the completion of order disposition, the firm can evaluate the performance of the shop floor against the standards in terms of such measures as:

The number of labor-hours used.

The breakdown of labor-hours between regular time and overtime.

The materials used by the order.

The number of hours of setup time required.

The amount of tooling required.

The date on which the order was completed.

The amount of rework or scrap generated by the order.

The number of machine-hours required.

The number of units completed.

This information is used by various departments in the firm and forms the basis for various cost-based reports. It also enables management to identify longer-term problems on the shop floor (e.g., the persistent lack of demonstrated capacity) and to modify cost and production standards.

# CHAPTER TWO

# Prerequisites to an Effective PAC System

Any PAC system, irrespective of the production setting in which it is found, must carry out the five major activities described in the previous chapter. The presence of these activities alone, however, is not enough to ensure an effective PAC system. Such a system is one that is able to execute all the plans released to it in a timely, efficient, and cost-effective manner. The effectiveness of any PAC system is ultimately dependent on (1) the existence of an effective formal manufacturing planning system, (2) the existence of a manufacturing data base containing all of the information needed by the PAC system to plan and control the flow of orders on the floor, and (3) the existence of a formal interface between the planning system and the PAC system. These three elements are prerequisites to an effective PAC system. That is, although a PAC system can operate in the absence of these elements, it can never operate *effectively* in their absence.

## THE MANUFACTURING PLANNING SYSTEM

The importance of the manufacturing planning system to the PAC system is based on three "principles" of PAC:

- The PAC system does not set plans; it carries out the plans and directions formulated in the planning system.

- The PAC system determines and controls operation priorities, not order priorities.
- The PAC system manages shop floor resources (machine capacity, tooling, material, and personnel); it does not acquire them.

The PAC system depends on the manufacturing planning system for direction and resources. The PAC system also depends on the manufacturing planning system for information on changes in order priorities. In short, the PAC system depends on the planning system for answers to these questions:

What products to build.
How many of the products to build.
When the products are needed.
What types of products are being built (i.e., are they for customers, or are they for safety stock replenishment?).

For the PAC system to be effective, the manufacturing planning system must meet three requirements:

1. *The planning system must be complete and integrated.* At a minimum, the manufacturing planning system must contain a production plan, a master production schedule, a material planning system, and a capacity planning system. (MRP is an example of a material planning system, and CRP is an example of a capacity planning system.) Furthermore, these components should be integrated. The plans generated by the material planning system should be consistent with the plans generated by the capacity planning system. These plans, in turn, should be consistent with the production objectives set down in the master production schedule (a detailed disaggregation of the production plan). Finally, the production plan should be a statement of manufacturing's commitment to corporate objectives.

Meeting this first requirement ensures that the planning system is responsible for the acquisition and disbursement of all the resources needed by the PAC system. It also ensures that the various plans are consistent both with one another and with the overall objectives of the firm.

2. *The planning system must be formal.* All of the production requirements inputted into and used by the PAC system must originate from the planning system. No requirements originating

outside the formal planning system should be placed on the PAC system.

3. *The planning system must generate valid and feasible plans for the PAC system.* For a PAC system to be effective, all the plans generated and released to it by the planning system must be valid and feasible. That is, these plans must accurately embody the objectives that the manufacturing planning system wishes to accomplish (i.e., the plans must be valid) and the PAC system must have access to the levels of resources needed in each planning period to execute the plans (i.e., the plans must be feasible).

The PAC system can maintain the validity of order priorities on an ongoing basis. It can ensure that the order need date conveyed by the planning system is equivalent to the order due date used on the shop floor when scheduling. This capability is mechanical. However, the PAC system cannot maintain the integrity of orders. Only the planning system can ensure that order priorities reflect what must be produced. The planning system is also responsible for managing dependent priority items. That is, the planning system (through MRP, for example) is responsible for coordinating the priorities of parent and component orders (vertical dependency) as well as the priorities of orders on the same level (horizontal dependency).

Furthermore, the PAC system does not have the capability of acquiring more resources should the current levels be insufficient. This capability belongs to the planning system alone. The function of the PAC system is to implement plans, not to acquire resources.

## THE MANUFACTURING DATA BASE

The term *manufacturing data base* describes a set of files that contain the information needed by the manufacturing system. Ideally, these files should be centrally located and part of a corporate data base. They can also be dispersed, with each function controlling the files of direct interest to it. For example, bills of materials or routing files might be located in the engineering department, while inventory item masters might be located in production and inventory control.

Irrespective of how the manufacturing data base is organized, it must satisfy certain minimal requirements:

- The data should be accurate (minimum acceptable level of accuracy—95 percent; should strive to maintain 100 percent accuracy or as close to 100 percent as possible).
- The data should be complete and should act as the source for the order documentation phase of the order review/release activities. The data should include information on tooling requirements, material requirements, and capacity requirements.
- The PAC system should have ready access to all necessary information.
- The data should be timely.
- The manufacturing data base should contain operational definitions for all the key terms used by the PAC system. The following should be among the terms defined:
  A work center
  Bills of material
  Routings
  Alternative routings
  Part family (if applicable)

## Structure of the Manufacturing Data Base

The PAC system depends on information to support its activities. This information is most commonly found in the following files:

1. Planning files
   Part (item) master file
   Tool master file
   Tool bill file
   Routing file
   Work center master
2. Control files
   Production order master file
   Shop order detail file

Planning files are crucial to the success of the order review/release activities of the PAC system. The planning files are used to evaluate and document orders. The control files are used to carry out the other PAC activities: establishment of operation priorities, shop reporting, and order control.

## Planning Files

The part master file is one of the most frequently used files in most manufacturing systems. It is used for inventory management, cost estimation, and PAC and by such formal material planning systems as MRP. Its purpose is to record in one file all of the data relevant to a specific part. For each part, there is one record. That record should contain the following data fields:

- *Part Number.* The unique number assigned to the item.
- *Part Description.* The name of the item.
- *Manufacturing Lead Time.* The normal time required to produce the item (for a typical lot size).
- *On-Hand Quantity.* The quantity of the item that is currently in stock.
- *Allocated Quantity.* The quantity of the item that is currently assigned (and as yet to be withdrawn) to previously planned future orders.
- *On-Order Quantity.* The number of units ordered (and in process) but not yet received from orders for the item.
- *Available Quantity.* The difference between the on-hand quantity and the allocated quantity. The number of units available to satisfy future orders for the item.
- *Manufacturing Lot Size Quantity.* The normal order quantity for the item.
- *Scrap Factor.* The amount of anticipated scrap. The scrap factor can be expressed as a percentage of the order, or it can be stated in terms of volume (e.g., 15 units). It can be broken down into the scrap allowance for setup and the "run time" scrap allowance.
- *Substitute Items.* The part numbers of items (or materials) that may be used in place of the item.
- *"Where Used" Fields.* The part numbers of the parent items using the item.
- *Specific Information Fields.* Fields may be set aside that contain information on such matters as the minimum lead time (the smallest time period in which the item can be realistically produced), minimum and maximum order quantities, order quantity multiples, and safety stock levels.

The second major planning file required by the PAC system is the *routing file*. The routing file consists of a set of records for each manufactured part. There is a separate record for each part and operation. The operation records are stored by manufacturing operation sequence. The purpose of the routing file is to store all of the information pertaining to the actions needed during the fabrication or assembly of an item. For each part, this file defines the sequence of the production events and the alternative events required to manufacture a product. The file may also contain records pertaining to such special manufacturing actions as subcontract operations, alternative operations, and special handling. Routing files are used to schedule operations and to calculate standard load-hours for capacity planning. The following fields are most frequently needed by the PAC system:

- *Operation Number.* The number assigned to a specific operation. Typically, such numbers are assigned in ascending sequence, reflecting the standard method of processing the item.
- *Operation Description.*
- *Abbreviated Standardized Operational Description Table Code.* A code that may be assigned to reduce verbal input.
- *Processing Department.* The department in which the operation is to be performed. Frequently, this department is identified by means of a code number or a description, or both.
- *Function/Work Center.* The function or work center in the department at which the operation is to be performed.
- *Machine Number.* A specific machine can be identified as being the most appropriate for performing the operation. The machine number may be the asset number assigned by accounting.
- *Setup Hours.* The standard time required to prepare equipment for the operation.
- *Standard Time per Piece.* The standard time required to process a predetermined number of items. That time may be expressed in such terms as standard time per piece, per 100 pieces, or per 1,000 pieces.
- *Standard Lot Sizing.* The number of pieces normally produced per run.
- *Tooling Required.* A description (using either a code num-

ber or a brief summary) of the kind and amount of tooling required for the operation.

- *Codes to Distinguish Types of Operations.* A set of codes may be used to provide the user with the following information:

    a. *Timed or Estimated Rates.* A code set at the time that the standard setup and run times are established to indicate the method used in arriving at the rate.

    b. *Regular or Alternative Operation.* A code to indicate whether the operation is the regular method or an alternative.

    c. *Multimachine Operation.* A code to specify the number of machines used for the operation or a code to specify the number of machines that an operator may employ simultaneously.

    d. *Subcontract Operation.* A code used to distinguish an operation that is to be performed by an outside vendor.

    e. *Special Handling.* A code to indicate whether any special handling conditions are to be observed when performing the operation.

The routings generated by the routing file are often supplemented by detail process sheets and process prints.

The third major planning file needed by PAC is the *work center master file*. This file assigns one record to each work center in the plant. Its purpose is to bring together all of the relevant information pertaining to a given work center. Like the routing file, the work center master file is used extensively in scheduling operations and in calculating standard load-hours for capacity planning. The following data are most often used by the PAC system:

- *Work Center Number.* The identification number of the work center.
- *Work Center Description.* A brief description of the work center and its composition.
- *Capacity Data.*
    a. Number of shifts per week.
    b. Number of machine-hours per week.
    c. Number of labor-hours per week.

- *Alternative Work Center.* The identification number of a work center that can be used in the event of machine breakdowns or *temporary* work center overloads.
- *Efficiency.* The ratio of actual performance to standard (expected) performance. Performance can be measured in terms of either labor-hours or machine-hours.
- *Utilization.* The percentage of time that a machine, work center, or line is available for work. The difference between the total number of hours and the number of hours of availability is due to such factors as equipment failure, tooling breakdown, lack of material, and scheduled downtime.
- *Effective Daily Capacity (EDC).* The number of standard hours of output that can be expected daily from a department. This measure is used both in evaluating the work center and in loading the work center with standard hours of work. Typically, it is calculated by multiplying the number of shifts per day times the number of hours per shift times efficiency times utilization.
- *Queue Time.* The *planned* number of hours that a typical job waits at the work center before processing is begun on it.
- *Specific Machine Constraints.* Constraints in the number of items that can be processed at one time or in the number of hours that a machine can be run at one time.

In addition to these three planning files, the PAC system may require a set of tooling-related planned files in those instances where tooling is a major and expensive resource. Tooling is most frequently a concern of companies that are involved in heavy fabrication (e.g., stamping, hobbing, grinding, turning, broaching, milling, and gun and rifle drilling) and that use:

Long lead time replacement tools.
High-cost tools.
A large number of duplicate tools.
Non-company-owned tools.

Under these circumstances, the PAC system will need the following planning files to control the use of the tooling resources:

Tool masters
Tool bills

The tool master contains all of the information relevant to the tooling used in the firm. There is one record for each tool controlled. The following data are especially relevant to the PAC system:

- *Tool Number.* The code number assigned to the tool.
- *Tool Description.* A brief description of the tool.
- *Tool Location.* The location of the tool. This can be stated in terms of a department code number, a work center code number, or a specific stockroom location. It should be the home location of the tool (i.e., the location to which the tool is to be returned after use).
- *Ownership Status.* This identifies whether or not the tool is owned by the firm.
- *Time between Rework/Disposal.* The number of pieces that a tool can be used to process before it is to be taken in for rework or disposal.
- *Number of Tools.* How many of the particular kind of tool are available for use.
- *Acquisition Cost.*
- *Date of Acquisition.* When the tool was acquired. Useful for determining when to replace or rework the tool.
- *Lead Time for Acquisition.* The number of days/weeks/ months needed to replace the tool.

The tool bill, like the routing file, identifies the tooling required for each part by operation. There is a separate record for each operation requiring tooling. The tooling records are stored in operation number sequence. The following data should be available for PAC:

- *Operation Number.* Same as that used in the routing file.
- *Tool Number.* The tooling, identified by number, required by the operation.

These two files can help the user in operation scheduling and in assessing tooling availability.[1]

---

[1]For more information on the effective management of tooling within the manufacturing system, see W. R. Wassweiler, "Tool Requirements Planning," *American Production and Inventory Control Society 25th Annual Conference Proceedings* (Falls Church, VA: American Production and Inventory Control Society, 1982), pp. 160–62.

## Control Files

Control files are used in recording and monitoring the progress of orders released to the shop floor. The first control file frequently used by the PAC system is the *production order master file.*

The production order master file contains a record on each active production order. The purpose of the file is to store summary data pertaining to the order's status, cost, priority, and nature. It contains the following data required by PAC:

- *Production Order Number.* The unique number assigned to the given production order.
- *Order Quantity.* The quantity (measured in units, pounds, bins, or gallons) to be produced on this order.
- *Quantity Completed.* The number of units reported finished through the last operation.
- *Quantity Scrapped.* The number of units scrapped for all operations on this order. Frequently, the amount of scrap incurred during setup and the amount of scrap incurred during production are kept on separate records.
- *Quantity Disbursed.* The quantity of all material issued to this order from stores.
- *Order Due Date.* The date by which the order is scheduled to be completed. Occasionally, this field may be broken into two separate fields. The first field is used to enter the *original* due date. This date, once entered, is never changed. The second field is used to enter the *revised* order due date. This field is used during rescheduling.
- *Priority.* A value calculated either by the system or manually using a predetermined logic (e.g., dispatching rule) and employed in ranking the order relative to other orders at any given work center.[2]
- *Balance Due.* The order quantity minus the number of items already completed and received (quantity completed) and the number of items scrapped (quantity scrapped). This field is frequently monitored by either the manufacturing planning system or the PAC system to determine whether an additional order should be released to

---

[2] The various methods of identifying these priorities are discussed in greater detail in Chapter Five.

make up an order shortcoming resulting from an excessively high scrap rate.

The *shop order detail file* is the second major control file extensively used by the PAC system. This file stores all planning, scheduling, progress, and priority data related to operations on shop orders. It is organized into a set of records, each of which pertains to a specific operation on a given shop order. The following fields are especially important to the PAC system:

- *Operation Number.* The unique number assigned to a specific operation.
- *Setup Hours Reported.* The actual number of hours, as reported, needed to set up the equipment for this operation on the given order.
- *Run Hours Reported.* The actual number of hours reported for processing the order through this operation.
- *Quantity Reported Complete.* The number of "good" (acceptable) pieces reported as completed through this operation.
- *Quantity Reported Scrapped.* The number of pieces reported as scrapped through this operation. This information can be broken down into the number of pieces reported as scrapped during setup and the number of pieces reported as scrapped during processing.
- *Due Date (Revised) or Lead Time Remaining.* This field contains the operation priority. That priority can be based either on the operation due date or on the lead time remaining (minimum slack). This information is used in assessing the relative priorities of the various competing shop orders.

## THE EXISTENCE OF A FORMAL INTERFACE FOR THE PAC SYSTEM

The final prerequisite for an effective PAC system is the existence of a formal interface between the PAC system and the manufacturing planning system. A method must be present whereby the PAC system can be made aware of relevant changes in the planning system and can keep the planning system aware of important changes taking place on the shop floor. As soon as changes in order need dates, order quantities, and order start dates are noted and recorded by the planning system, they must be communicated to the people in the PAC system so that these people can make the appropriate revisions in operation priorities. Similarly, changes on the shop floor affecting the operation of the planning system (e.g., an excessively high scrap rate or a machine breakdown delaying the completion of a needed component) must be reported back to the planning system so that appropriate adjustments to plans can be made.

To conduce to the presence of an effective PAC system, the interface must be *formal* and ongoing. The development of such an interface can be encouraged in various ways:

- By using data that are accessible to both the manufacturing planning system and the PAC system.
- By ensuring that all plans produced by the PAC system are distributed to the appropriate PAC personnel.
- By ensuring that the format employed to record information on the shop floor is useful to both the PAC system and the manufacturing planning system.

# CHAPTER THREE

# Structuring the Production Activity Control System

To be effective, any PAC system, irrespective of the specific manufacturing setting in which it is used, must have in place the three prerequisites discussed in Chapter 2. Any PAC system must also comprise the five major activities discussed in Chapter 1. But how the PAC system for a specific firm is best structured (i.e., how the PAC activities are carried out and their importance) is largely determined by the characteristics, practices, and requirements of the manufacturing process.

Production can take place in a wide range of settings. These settings occupy a continuum that can be broken down into three major categories:

1. Project manufacturing.
2. Job shop (discrete batch) manufacturing.
3. Repetitive/continuous manufacturing.

This book will focus on the second and third categories since most of its readers will have systems falling into these categories. First, the structuring of the PAC system for the job shop will be described. Then, the structuring of the PAC system for repetitive/continuous manufacturing systems will be described in terms of the changes that must be made in the job shop PAC system.

## STRUCTURING PAC FOR THE JOB SHOP

PAC systems operating in job shop settings must be structured to accommodate the following important manufacturing characteristics:

1. Product design, process requirements, and order quantity are extremely variable.
2. Order flows on the shop floor seldom have the straight-line continuity of order flow that is observed in repetitive/continuous manufacturing systems.
3. To accommodate the extensive variability in orders, general-purpose machines are ordinarily used. These machines are grouped into work centers consisting of similar or identical machines (an arrangement that is frequently referred to as a "functional layout").
4. The setup time component of manufacturing lead time is quite significant relative to the per unit processing time. Lot sizing is therefore often used to balance the setup and holding costs.
5. Capacity is difficult to plan in advance because the actual capacity needed depends on such factors as the mix of orders in the shop and the sequence in which the orders are processed at the various work centers.
6. Queue time is an important element of the overall manufacturing lead time. In most job shops, a typical order spends between 90 and 95 percent of its lead time waiting in queues.

Manufacturing lead times are a critical concern of the PAC systems operating in job shops. In general, PAC spends a great of its time controlling and managing manufacturing lead times.

## MANUFACTURING LEAD TIMES: AN OVERVIEW

Manufacturing lead times are very important to all job shops. They influence nearly every aspect of the planning and operation of job shops. Manufacturing lead times (planned and actual) are used during capacity, material, and priority planning. They affect the amount of work-in-process, safety stock levels, and reorder points (if used). Finally, they influence the firm's strategic stance, for as manufacturing lead times increase, the firm's flexibility decreases. For the firm to be successful, the PAC system must manage and control manufacturing lead times.

Briefly defined, manufacturing lead time is the time that elapses between the release of the order to the shop floor and the completion of all operations on the order and its receipt into stock. Manufacturing lead time can be divided into two basic categories:

- *Operation Time.* The time during which the order is processed on a machine. This includes setup time and production time.
- *Interoperation Time.* The time that the order is involved in nonproduction activities on the shop floor (e.g., being moved and waiting in queue).

The major components of interoperation time are:

- *Queue Time.* The time that the order spends waiting at a machine or a work center before being processed.
- *Preparation Time.* The time required to complete work that must be done before the operation can begin. Components of preparation time include time spent in cleaning, heating, or marking out the part.
- *Postoperation Time.* Production activity that takes place at the end of an operation and that imposes no load on the work center. Examples of such activity include cooling, cleaning, deburring, wrapping, and local inspection.
- *Wait Time.* Time that the order spends waiting for transportation to the next work center.
- *Transportation Time.* Time that the order spends moving between work centers.

Queue time is the largest and most important of these components, typically accounting for between 90 and 95 percent of the total manufacturing lead time for an order.

The general composition of manufacturing lead time is illustrated in Figure 4. In general, operation time depends on order characteristics (e.g., the order quantity, the number of processes to be completed), while interoperation time depends on conditions in the shop (e.g., the existing load, the nature of the load, the rate of order release). Interoperation time is longer in dura-

**FIGURE 4** Elements of Manufacturing Lead Time

| Queue time | Preparation time | Post-operation time | Wait time | Transportation time | Setup time | Production time |
|---|---|---|---|---|---|---|
| | | Interoperation time | | | Operation time | |

←———————————————— Manufacturing lead time ————————————————→

tion than operation time and also the primary source of lead time variability.

In the job shop, PAC is responsible for lead time management and reduction. That is, PAC must reduce the average lead time and the degree of variability around this mean value. It must highlight any inflation in lead times and identify and eliminate the underlying causes. Given the importance of queue times, the task of lead time management can be reduced to the task of queue time (or queue) control. As can be seen from Figure 5, PAC works at creating the queues shown in A. Unlike the queues depicted in B (which suffer from excessive lead time inflation due to an unnecessary buffer of 80 hours), C (which are plagued by excessive variability in queue time), and D (which are chronically underloaded), the queues in A are relatively tight (i.e., they have low variability around the mean) and do not suffer from underloading or overloading.

PAC controls lead times and queues by controlling and monitoring the rates at which orders enter and are processed through work centers. PAC continuously tries to match the workload (the inputs) with the work capacity (the potential rate of work flow through a work center or department) and to identify and correct any deviations in this match. This focus is illustrated in Figure 6. In all effective PAC systems, the PAC activities deal extensively with establishing and maintaining the match between the workload and the work capacity.

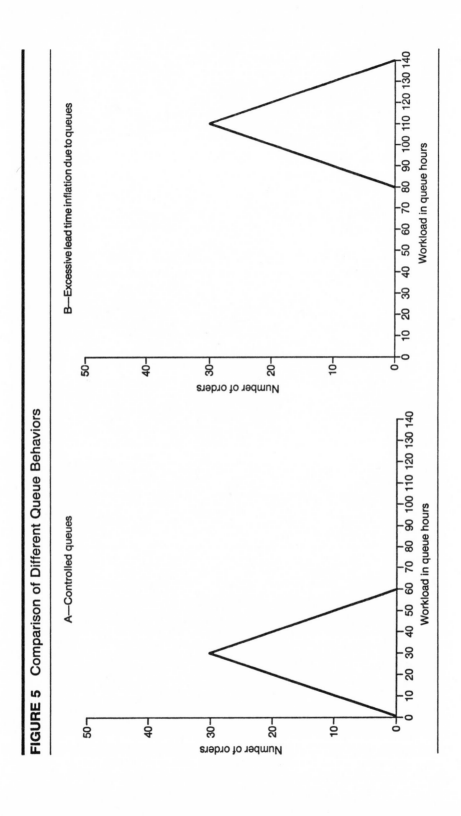

**FIGURE 5** Comparison of Different Queue Behaviors

**FIGURE 5** *(concluded)*

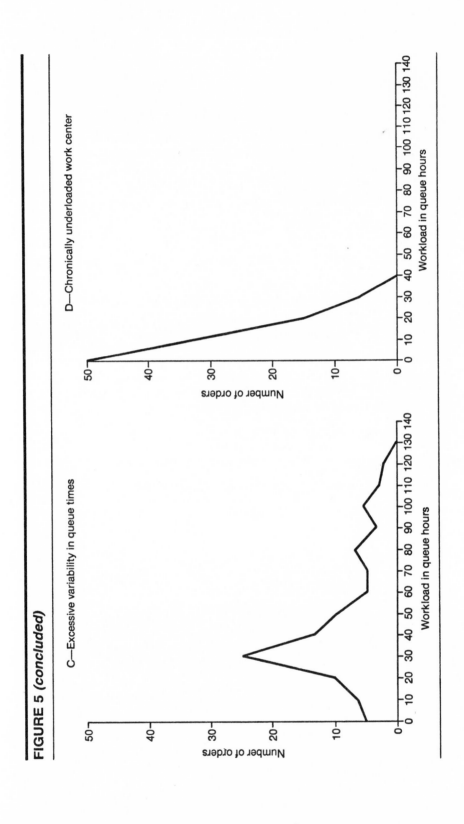

C—Excessive variability in queue times

D—Chronically underloaded work center

## FIGURE 6  PAC—Controlling Queues and Workload

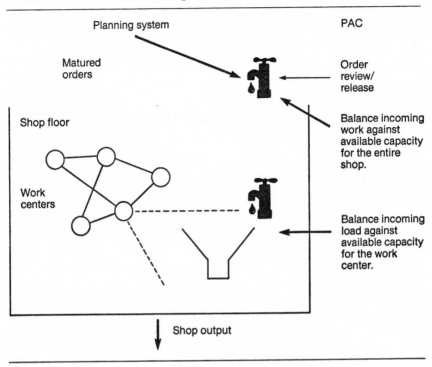

# CHAPTER FOUR

# PAC Activities in the Job Shop: Order Review/Release

Order review/release is the first major activity of production activity control. This activity is responsible for managing the movement of an order from the planning system to the shop floor. Once the order has been released to the shop floor, it can be properly regarded as a *work authorization.* It authorizes shop floor personnel to allocate shop floor resources (personnel, material, tooling, and machine capacity) against the order. It also forms the basic document for control.

## PURPOSES OF ORDER REVIEW/RELEASE

Order review/release has three basic purposes:

1. Order preparation.
2. Review and evaluation of orders.
3. Control of work flow to the shop floor.

The first purpose is straightforward. Order review/release is responsible for ensuring that the order released by the planning system contains all of the information required by shop floor personnel. This activity includes documentation (as previously described in this book), attachment of appropriate drawings (if necessary), and assignment of a shop order number (if this number has not been assigned previously).

The second purpose, review and evaluation of orders, is a far more critical and important activity. During the order review/release stage, every order to be released to the shop floor *must* be reviewed and evaluated. Potential problems in capacity, tooling or material availability, or lead time viability should be identified at this stage, and the order affected by these problems should be kept off the shop floor until the problems have been resolved. Only orders that have a "good" chance of being completed on time should be released to the shop floor. Thus, order review/release should act as a *filter*.

By controlling the rate at which orders flow to the shop floor (the third purpose), order review/release helps PAC control queues and reduce congestion on the shop floor. As a general rule, the shop floor operates most effectively when the number of jobs present on it is held to a minimum.

## EVENTS TRIGGERING ORDER REVIEW/RELEASE

Order review/release is typically initiated for the following reasons:

1. Planned order release recommended by the MRP system.
2. Scrap replacement before MRP generates the appropriate planned order.
3. Compensation for yield or shrink before MRP detects the need and issues the appropriate planned order.
4. Anticipation of impending demand before the MPS is increased.
5. Overcoming delays caused by rework.
6. Anticipated scrap.
7. Load leveling prior to MRP adjustments.
8. Management edict. This is any order or production schedule that is released to the PAC system at the insistence of management. Such orders do not reflect actual need as identified either in the planning system or on the shop floor. Examples of management edict orders are the issuance of work for a machine in order to demonstrate its capabilities for management and the issuance of work in order to keep an area of the plant busy.

In general, order review/release activities should be initiated by the formal planning system. These activities may be triggered directly by a planned order release (order type 1 in the preceding list), or they may be triggered in anticipation of an action to be taken by the formal planning system. The PAC system must be linked on an ongoing basis to the formal planning system. This linkage ensures that the PAC system operates only on those orders *actually* required by the planning system and that any changes in order priorities reflect changes in planning system requirements.

For these reasons, management edicts should be treated with caution. Such orders are not linked to the planning system; they have not been planned for by the planning system; and in many instances their impact (in terms of material, capacity, and tooling) has not been evaluated by the planning system. As a rule, they should be avoided whenever possible and they should be released to the PAC system on an *exception* basis.

## AUTHORITY FOR ORDER REVIEW/RELEASE

There is one major rule of effective order review/release: *Every order released to the PAC system for completion should be reviewed and evaluated by someone who is held responsible for controlling the flow of orders to the shop floor. Orders should never be automatically released to the shop floor.* One major reason for the poor operation of many PAC systems is the failure to strictly follow this rule.

When the planning system authorizes the release of orders to the shop floor, it cannot be expected to be aware of all the conditions on the shop floor that affect the processing of orders. Furthermore, the planning system cannot be expected to keep pace with all of the changes (e.g., machine breakdowns, absent workers) on the shop floor. PAC personnel must be entrusted to keep track of information from the shop floor and to use that information when reviewing and releasing orders.

Typically, responsibility for order review/release is assigned either to individuals working together in a department or to a release committee. An individual can be assigned to review orders whose release does not require the cooperation of other departments. Individuals who perform this function are assigned such titles as production controllers (Bently-Nevada), production control analysts (Moog), or parts planners. (Later in the chapter, we will use the term *parts planner* to identify the PAC person responsible for reviewing planned orders and authorizing the release of orders to the shop floor.) A release committee is necessary when the cooperation of more than one department is required. A good example of a release committee is the JIT (Just-in-Time) Committee at the Consumer Healthcare Division, Miles Laboratories. This committee brings together representatives from Quality Assurance, Warehousing, Material Planning, and Finished Goods Planning. It reviews the production schedules to be released to the PAC system for the upcoming week. A major reason for the existence of this committee is that the material required by the shop floor must first clear Quality Assurance. The JIT Committee provides the PAC system with one means of prioritizing the actions of Quality Assurance. Materials that are needed next week for production but have not yet cleared Quality Assurance or have not yet been received are identified during the JIT Committee meetings, and appropriate action is taken. The JIT Committee also helps coordinate the activities of Quality Assurance with the needs of the shop floor.

Irrespective of how the authority for order review/release is assigned, certain characteristics should be present in this function:

- Familiarity with the operation of the planning system and an ability to interpret and understand the reports generated by this system.
- Familiarity with the operation of the PAC system and an ability to interpret the reports generated by this system.
- Awareness of current conditions on the shop floor.
- Accountability for managing the movement of orders from the planning system to the shop floor.
- Ability to change the release dates of orders to best utilize the shop floor resources.

The order review/release function should not operate in isolation. It must cooperate on an ongoing basis with people from both the shop floor and the planning system. The cooperation of these two groups is required in order to identify and resolve any potential problems affecting the release of orders to the shop floor.

## INFORMATION FLOWS AND FORMS

The flow of information from the planning system to the PAC system and from the PAC system to the shop floor can take numerous forms. These forms can be broken down into three major categories:

1. Verbal releases.
2. Hard copy.
3. Paperless (on-line systems).

Of these three categories, verbal releases are the least desirable. Such releases, most commonly used in small shops, can be as simple as verbal instructions conveyed from the owner or the manager to PAC personnel. They suffer from several significant limitations and problems. Information may be inaccurately and incompletely conveyed—the information received on the shop floor is often not the information that the manager wished to convey. More important, there is no written record of what information was communicated and when the order was actually released. In short, it is difficult to evaluate performance, control the job shop, or enforce strict accountability of shop floor personnel when orders are issued from the planning system on the basis of verbal information *alone*.

For most firms, information is most commonly communicated by means of some form of hard copy. Order release information can be produced using handwritten forms. In most instances, the information is contained on computer-printed forms. In many firms, such forms are produced on a regular basis (at least once a week) by a formal material planning system such as MRP.

Increasingly, "paperless" systems are being employed. In these systems, the PAC system can access on-line, real-time information by means of a computer (CRT) terminal. Paperless systems offer several important advantages over verbal and hard copy systems. It is easier to maintain informational accuracy with paperless systems since changes to the manufacturing data can be made on-line, thus generating the changes almost immediately. Changes in order status can be quickly conveyed to the affected parties. In short, on-line systems provide users with access to the most current information. Users of such systems are not plagued by the time delays present in other systems (i.e., the intervals between the time when a change takes place and the time when information regarding that change is entered into the system and the appropriate reports are generated and distributed).

Paperless systems often generate hard copy reports. These reports are permanent records that can be taken away from the terminal by the user.

Order release reports generated by the planning system (or from the shop floor in anticipation of the planning system) can pertain to:

Individual orders (in the case of scrap, rework, or yield problems).

A group of orders (the form typically taken by planned order releases recommended by MRP).

Daily run schedules (most typically found in repetitive/continuous manufacturing systems).

Examples of such reports are found in Figure 7. In reviewing such reports, certain information, common to all order release forms, must be conveyed. At a minimum, these forms must contain:

Part number.

Job order number. (If not assigned by the planning system, this number will be assigned as part of the order review/release stage of PAC.)

Order due date.

Order type (scrap, rework, ordinary order).

Order quantity.

Recommended order release date.

Minimum order release date.

## REVIEW STEPS BEFORE RELEASE OF ORDER

On receiving a request for an order release, the person responsible for reviewing the order should complete the following review steps:

1. Stage the material on the computer to determine availability.[1]
2. Determine availability of capacity.
3. Determine availability of tooling.

---

[1]If the MRP system is operating effectively, this step can be omitted since the MRP system has assured the availability of adequate material.

---

**FIGURE 7** Examples of Order Release Reports

---

ATTACHMENT E

```
CICS8350  RPOR AUTH:    DATA:
FN: PELS               ORDER MAINTENANCE AND RELEASE
GEO LUL: SH
ITEM NO: 1278660            STOCK POT W/COV 20 QT          DATE: 08/04/85
ORDER NO: 0917869   ORDER STATUS: F
-----                                                   -----
DESCRIPTION                 DATA            COMMENTS
----------------------      ---------       --------------------------------
ORDER QUANTITY                  1,000
RELEASE DATE                08/04/xx        MUST BE VALID SHOP DATE
DUE DATE                    08/08/xx        MUST BE VALID SHOP DATE
PRODUCING LOCATION          STOCK
ORDER TYPE                  M
SHOP/PURCHASE ORDER NO.                     LOW-ORDER POSITION MUST = 0,
                                            FOR 'M' ORDERS
KEY OPERATION                               RELS - INDICATES BEGINNING
                                            OPERATION
                                            REPL - INDICATES FIRST
                                            OPERATION TO BE AFFECTED
----- RPOR50 CHECK ORDER DATA                                    -----
FUNCTION CODES: INQU - INQUIRY (DEFAULT)    ISRT - ADD NEW PLANNED ORDER
                FIRM - FIRM A PLANNED ORDER ISRV - ADD ORDER W COMPONENTS
                RELS - RELEASE ORDER        REPL - UPDATE ORDER
                DLET - DELETE ORDER         REPV - UPDATE ORDER w VERIFY
```

---

4. Determine availability of current routing and process information to support start date and order or lot size.
5. Review the MRP printout for:
   a. Reasonableness of lot size.
   b. Lead time accuracy.
   c. Viability of planned lead time in relationship to the need date.
   d. Assignment of order number if not assigned by the planning system.
   e. Coding of the order as:

**FIGURE 7** *(concluded)*

Moog SFC SWAN Log

| SWAN | PART NUMBER | DESC (NOT PCHD) | PRINT CHNG | DUE DATE | ORDER QUANTITY | MODEL | CHRG TO | AUTHORIZATION | DEPT | MACH | DETL LOAD |
|------|-------------|-----------------|------------|----------|----------------|-------|---------|---------------|------|------|-----------|
| 124792A | A22615-001 | GLAND | | 259 | 100 | 17-335C | O | | 84D | | D |
| 124800A | A22714-003 | HSG | | 307 | 35 | 17-335C | O | | 72A | | D |
| 124818A | A22714-005 | HSG | | 307 | 35 | 17-335C | O | | 72A | | D |
| 124826A | A44070-001 | END CAPASM | | 219 | 100 | 17-341 | O | | 72A | | D |
| 124834A | A44361-001 | BODY | | 265 | 20 | 17-354A | O | | 73A | | D |
| | | | | | | | | | | | |
| | | | | | | | | | | | |
| | | | | | | | | | | | |
| | | | | | | | | | | | |
| | | | | | | | | | | | |

DATE 8-15-83  BY P.Q.

(1) Rework.

(2) Customer.

(3) Stock.

This information can be used when assigning operation priorities. In general, when there is a conflict in priorities, customer orders should be given preference over rework orders and orders to stock.

   *f.* Review the shrink factor for accuracy. The shrink factor, which can be expressed either as a percentage of the order quantity (e.g., 15 percent) or as a quantity (e.g., 100 pieces), should be reviewed before the order is released. Under certain conditions (e.g., suspect material, new operators, a new production process or work method, or a new part), the shrink factor should be increased to reflect greater uncertainty. The person responsible for reviewing orders should draw on his experience when evaluating the shrink factor.

g.  Review the MRP production schedules to identify potential opportunities for improving the operation of the shop by releasing a family of part numbers. A family of part numbers can consist of orders sharing either common setups or common components.

h.  Review the GT (group technology) code, if applicable, to identify opportunities for releasing items belonging to the same GT part family.

i.  Review pegged requirements if necessary. This review is undertaken in cases where the order initially specified in the planned order release cannot be successfully completed on the shop floor. The purpose of the review is to identify alternative order quantities that can be released. For example, if the initial order quantity is the result of lot sizing, the order quantity can be split or it can be reduced to match the exact needs of the parent as indicated in the pegged requirements.

6.  Make any necessary modifications to the bill of material for a specific shop order

7.  Make any necessary modifications in routing for a specific shop order

8.  Identify and evaluate the impact of any engineering changes on the shop order

9.  Evaluate the impact on current shop floor resources of increasing the lot size of an existing order as an alternative to releasing an additional shop order

10.  Identify and evaluate the impact on the schedule of orders whose purpose is safety stock replenishment. Not all orders are equally important; orders intended to satisfy customer demands should receive a higher priority than orders intended primarily to replenish partly consumed safety stock. If currently available shop resources are inadequate to process all orders, then orders whose purpose is safety stock replenishment should be carefully reviewed and only those that can be accommo-

dated after customer orders have been accommodated should be released. Since such orders are *not* directly linked to customer orders, their release can be delayed if necessary.

These review steps help the user assign planned order releases into one of two categories:

1. Those that can be released to the shop floor.
2. Those that cannot be released.

Orders that have access to adequate capacity, material, and tooling and that have viable lead times and reasonable scrap factors and lot sizes belong to the first category: these orders have a "good" chance of being completed on time. The parts planners can now prepare the shop documentation in anticipation of the release of such orders to the shop floor.

The second category comprises orders that face one or more problems. These problems are frequently a result of inadequate capacity, inadequate material, or too short a planned lead time. The problems must be corrected before an order in this category can be released to the shop floor. Typically, the necessary corrective actions require the cooperation of personnel from both the PAC system and the planning system. These actions may include:

Rescheduling the order's due date.
Lot splitting.
Adding more short-term capacity (through overtime or an extra shift).
Subcontracting the order.

Under certain conditions, a problem order may be released to the shop floor based on the assertion that the problem will be corrected before it is encountered on the shop floor. This type of order is usually referred to as a *forced release.*

## FORCED RELEASE ORDERS

In general, "shorted" orders (orders with *currently* insufficient inventory in one or more component parts) are kept off the shop floor until adequate inventory becomes available. This delay is reflected in the planned released date, and it may become reflected in the order due date if the order has to be rescheduled by the planning system to accommodate the change in release date. Forced release is the only exception to this practice of keeping "shorted" orders off the shop floor.

Under certain conditions, a shorted order may be released to the shop floor for processing. Typically, these conditions include:

- Shortages involving material that has been delayed (either at the vendors or in the shop) but is expected to arrive before the time at which it is needed by the order.
- Shortages that can be filled by recovering component salvage.
- Shortages in which off-standard material can be used to fill the order.
- Situations in which capacity is currently available for the order but may not be available in the future. In this instance, the missing components may be subsequently added at a higher cost.

Under these conditions, the shorted order may be released to the shop floor. The order is noted as being shorted, and stores (and, in some instances, shop floor personnel) is warned that certain components are missing. Where off-standard material is used, stores makes the substitutions. Where material is missing, stores does not attempt to locate it (the stores personnel know in advance that it is missing). When the material arrives, stores records it and immediately sends it to the order on the shop floor.

In general, a forced release exposes the PAC system to numerous potential problems. The parts planner is taking a calculated risk. He is betting that the material will arrive before it is needed. If it does not, shop floor resources that other orders could have been use committed to an order that is now idle on the shop floor. Thus, the parts planner should review each forced release carefully. He must accept the responsibility for any forced release, authorizing such orders manually (the parts planner must be willing to "sign off" on them).

## PREPARATION OF THE SHOP ORDER PACKET/TRAVELER

The final stage before releasing an order to the shop floor involves the preparation of the shop order documentation (frequently referred to as the *shop packet* or *traveler*). Like the planned order, the shop packet can be generated and distributed in hard copy form or transmitted as a paperless transaction. (The current trend is toward the increased usage of paperless or on-line transactions.) In either case, the shop packet must provide shop floor personnel with the following:

1. *Material Requisitions.* The material requisition is an authorization to withdraw the necessary component items from stores. The withdrawal can be done either by stores personnel or by the shop personnel to whom the order has been assigned. In either case, stores personnel should receive a copy of the material requisition so that they are warned of the forthcoming withdrawal. The material requisition is frequently called the *picking list*.

2. *Tooling Requisitions.* Like the material requisition, the tooling requisition is an authorization allowing shop personnel to withdraw and use specific tooling to complete the order. If tooling is kept in a tooling stores, the tooling stores personnel should receive a copy of the tooling requisition.

3. *Manufacturing Routing Sheets.* The information contained on these sheets has been previously described in this book.

4. *Shop Order Identification Cards.*

5. *Drawing and/or NC Tapes.* The shop packet can either contain the necessary drawings and NC tapes or provide shop personnel with requests for the appropriate drawing and tapes.

The information contained in the shop packet has been described in detail in the discussion of the manufacturing data base in Chapter Two. Once the complete shop packet has been generated, the parts planner can release the order to the shop floor. At this point, the order review/release phase of the PAC system has been completed.

## OTHER CONSIDERATIONS FOR ORDER REVIEW/RELEASE

In addition to the considerations discussed above, there are other considerations that should be taken into account in the order review/release phase. These considerations can be summarized as follows:

1. *The shop load from period to period should be as level as possible.*

2. *When smoothing the shop load, work should be pulled forward whenever possible.* In general, the shop load should be smoothed at the planning stage. Because of changes taking place on the shop floor, this smoothing is often inadequate. Management on the shop floor can smooth the shop load further by pulling work forward or by pushing work back. The preferred action is to pull work forward. Pushing work back can create severe problems for the manufacturing system by causing the rescheduling process to ripple clear up to the customer order level. Pushing work back tends to create more problems than it solves.

3. *The persons responsible for reviewing and releasing work should also monitor future workloads.* A major advantage offered by most modern formal material and capacity planning systems (such as MRP and CRP) is that they provide users with visibility over future workloads. This visibility is especially important to those involved in the order review/release phase of PAC. In general, the parts planners should concern themselves not only with matured orders in the current time bucket but also with the incoming workload for the next two to four weeks. Evaluation of future workloads provides warning. Any problems in capacity identified during such evaluation can be reacted to in advance by pulling work forward or by adding extra capacity in the form of overtime or an extra shift. By monitoring future workloads, the parts planner gives himself more time to react to upcoming problems.

After the order has been released to the shop floor, it becomes the focus of detailed scheduling, the next major set of PAC activities.

# CHAPTER FIVE

# PAC Activities in the Job Shop: Detailed Scheduling

Detailed scheduling—the process by which the various shop resources are matched with demand—is the activity that most people associate most closely with PAC. In the PAC system, the demand for shop resources comes from three major areas:

1. Shop orders.
2. Preventive maintenance.
3. Salvage and rework orders.

Each area requires its own process for detailed scheduling. In this chapter, the major focus of the discussion will be on the process of scheduling orders.

## SCHEDULING ORDERS

When we talk of scheduling orders (the primary focus of detailed scheduling), we are dealing mainly with the dispatching process. The dispatching process involves the assignment of priorities to orders waiting in queue at a given work center. Such assignment is not a mechanical process whereby a priority rule (otherwise referred to as a dispatching rule) is used to identify an order sequence that the operator implements *without deviation*. It is a process whereby the PAC system provides shop personnel with access to necessary information that they use to determine the exact sequence in which orders are to be processed. It is also a *controlled* process. The shop personnel can manipulate the priorities of orders *only* as long as these priorities satisfy certain criteria communicated by the PAC system. In short, the dispatching process is primarily a *people* process.

## Objectives of the Dispatching Process

In any job shop, the dispatching process should be structured to achieve at least the following objectives:

1.  To ensure that orders released to the shop floor are completed by the order due date.
2.  To improve the efficiency of the shop floor.
3.  To help maintain a level load across work centers.

In any formal manufacturing system (especially one operating MRP), the PAC system is continuously linked to the planning system by the order due date. This date forms a contract between the two systems. The planning system expects to receive the order by that date, and the PAC system is therefore responsible for ensuring that the order is completed by that date. The dispatching process must work toward this goal.

In most job shops, the order must go through a number of operations, each done at a different work center. For the order to be completed on time, each operation must be completed on time (by its operation due date). At each operation, a number of orders are competing to gain access to the resources offered by a work center. The dispatching process is responsible for sequencing these competing orders to support such PAC objectives as the on-time completion of orders. That is, the process tries to identify the sequence in which orders should be processed through a work center so that they become available by their operation due dates (and thus their order due dates).

At a minimum, the planning system should generate *feasible* plans. This means that the orders released by the planning system to the PAC system should not require access to more shop resources than are currently available. The schedules from the planning system are not necessarily efficient. Improved efficiency comes from the dispatching process. Efficiency results from regrouping orders at work centers so as to reduce load by taking advantage of similarities in components, processing, or setups.

The dispatching process should also be expected to maintain a level load across work centers. When work is scheduled at a given work center, the order of processing should reflect conditions not only at that work center but also at downstream work centers. Orders going to relatively idle work centers should have a higher priority than orders going to congested work centers. By scheduling away from bottleneck operations, the dispatching process helps to minimize order idle time and to control manufacturing lead times.

The dispatching process may also be held accountable for other objectives. These may include improving the cash flow generated on the shop floor by giving priority to high-revenue or high-profit orders or maintaining customer goodwill by giving priority to orders for large or favored customer accounts. However, the three objectives identified in this section are basic to all PAC systems.

## Organization and Staffing of the Dispatching Process

There are many different methods by which the dispatching process can be incorporated into the firm's PAC system. These methods can be best envisioned as occupying a spectrum (see Figure 8). At one extreme of the spectrum, there is *centralized* dispatching. Under this method of organization, all dispatching is done from one central location. Centralized dispatching offers two major advantages:

1. It requires less personnel than does assigning a dispatcher to each department.
2. It encourages communication among dispatchers, so that every dispatcher is aware of the latest order requirements as well as the condition of the shop.

Centralized dispatching is most appropriate to processes in which:

- The products are fairly standard and their processing characteristics are well known.
- There are a large number of like machines and labor skills, so that it is not important to which specific machine or worker a job is assigned.

---

**FIGURE 8** The Dispatching Spectrum

---

| *100 Percent Centralized* | *100 Percent Decentralized* |
| --- | --- |
| All dispatching done in one position | Dispatchers assigned to various departments and work centers |
| Communication primarily among dispatchers | Encourages communication among dispatchers, supervisors, and operators |
| Typically under a PIC manager and separate from the department supervisors and operators | Dispatchers work under either a general superintendent or a department supervisor |
| Most appropriate for standard products, automated processes, and situations in which there is little difference in labor and machines | Most appropriate for diverse products or products in which there are significant machine and labor differences |

---

- There are many short jobs and the order in which jobs are done does not matter too much as long as all jobs are done on time.
- There are no significant problems of sequence-dependent processing (i.e., it does not really matter in which order jobs are processed because the jobs all have very similar or very dissimilar setups, components, or processing requirements).
- The dispatchers are aware of significant sequence dependencies if there are any.
- There are automated processes.

At the other extreme, there is *decentralized* dispatching. In this case, the dispatching process is broken up and done by allowing the individual work areas (work centers, departments, or plants) to make their own decisions regarding the exact order in which the various jobs are to be processed. Decentralized dispatching requires more dispatchers, but it encourages greater cooperation and communication between the dispatcher and those working on the shop floor (specifically the department supervisor and machine operators). It also enables the dispatcher to develop a greater familiarity with the capabilities and limitations of the department to which he is assigned, its and with the fit between those capabilities and the orders assigned to the department.

Decentralization is most appropriate to situations in which:

- There are significant differences in machine capabilities or labor skills, so that the assignment of a job to a specific machine or worker could have a significant effect on the time and costs incurred in completing the job.
- There are significant sequence dependencies that the dispatchers are unaware of.
- The products are prototypes or very diverse or run very infrequently.
- There are many long jobs.

Most job shops fall somewhere between these extremes, so some mixture of centralized and decentralized dispatching is usually desirable.

For most PAC systems used in job shops, the dispatching process will involve three groups of people: the dispatchers, the department supervisors, and the operator. Each group brings important insights and information to the dispatching process, so the priorities ultimately assigned should reflect the inputs of these three groups.

The dispatcher in many PAC systems is typically part of the production and inventory control (PIC) function. He is therefore often expected to act as an interface between the PIC function and the shop floor. His major responsibilities include controlling the flow of work to the various work centers and providing shop personnel with a "recommended" set of order priorities (in the form of the *dispatch list*). The dispatcher's responsibilities typically include:

- Keeping the shop personnel aware of the status of work (e.g., orders to arrive, orders in queue and ready to be processed, orders assigned to the work center but not yet released, orders released and behind schedule).
- Controlling the flow of orders to the work center (i.e., to reduce the level of congestion and work-in-process on the shop floor).
- Keeping shop personnel aware of changes in order due dates.
- Keeping shop personnel constantly aware of past-due orders.

- Linking the PIC department to the shop floor on an ongoing basis.
- Acting as a liaison between the PAC system and the manufacturing planning system.
- Working with other dispatchers and the department supervisors to provide shop personnel with a timely and level flow of orders and material.
- Working with the department supervisor and, in cases where the knowledge of the operator is critical, the machine operator, in determining the actual priorities to be implemented at the various work centers.

The department supervisor is responsible for managing the allocation of the shop floor resources under his control to the various orders released to his department by the dispatcher. In achieving this task, the department supervisor must draw on his knowledge of his department and of the capabilities and limitations of the machines and workers. Typically, his responsibilities include:

- Determining which machine or operator is to work on a specific order.
- Monitoring the capacity levels of his department.
- Evaluating the feasibility of the orders released by the dispatcher in light of *current* conditions on the shop floor.
- Keeping the dispatcher aware of any anticipated delays in order completion (and the length of those delays).
- Ensuring that all transactions in his department pertaining to such areas as labor-hours worked, scrap, salvage, rework, downtime, setup time, and material usage are recorded in a timely fashion.
- Verifying that all transactions entries are accurate.
- Identifying the reasons for shop floor problems.
- Ensuring that all work released to his department is completed and made available by the due date.
- Working with the operator in determining the ultimate sequence of jobs.

The operator brings his knowledge of the process, the product, and the machine to the dispatching process. Ultimately, the operator is responsible for identifying the sequence that improves efficiency *without* compromising the operation date and the order due date. It is the operator who often does the "fine-tuning" to the recommended priorities, as communicated by the dispatch list. Typically, the operator's responsibilities include:

- Determining the actual sequence in which orders are to be processed.
- Monitoring capacity at his work center.
- Communicating any problems (e.g., machine breakdowns, excessive scrap) and anticipated delays in orders to the department supervisor.
- Identifying and recording the reasons for these problems (thus providing the PAC system with an information base for corrective actions).
- Evaluating and commenting on the feasibility of the workloads released to his work center.
- Working with other operators and the department supervisor to smooth the shop load by pulling work forward, when possible, to take advantage of similarities in setups, components, and processing.
- Monitoring the status of upstream and downstream work centers and using this information, when possible, to modify operation priorities (e.g., increasing the priority of orders going to relatively underutilized work centers and decreasing the priority of orders going to bottleneck operations).
- Recording in a timely and accurate fashion all of the transactions taking place at his work center.
- Meeting the schedules and due dates.

In nearly all job shops, none of these three people working by himself and in isolation can arrive at the best sequence of orders for a given work center. All three of them bring important information and insights to the dispatching process. Assigning work and determining priorities is a dynamic process that requires an ongoing interaction among these three people. The flow of information must go from the dispatcher to the department supervisor to the operator and back. The interactions among these three people are summarized in Figure 9.

---

**FIGURE 9** Dispatching Interactions

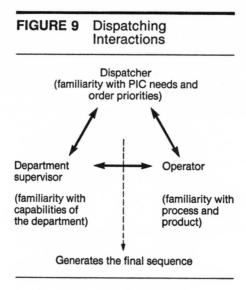

Dispatcher
(familiarity with PIC needs and
order priorities)

Department supervisor

(familiarity with capabilities of the department)

Operator

(familiarity with process and product)

Generates the final sequence

---

## Scheduling versus Detailed Sequencing

The dispatching process in any job shop involves two important activities: scheduling and detailed sequencing. These activities may be one and the same under certain conditions and distinct under other conditions. Scheduling involves assigning the jobs to be processed through a work center, department, or plant over a given time period (e.g., shift, day, or week) and determining the priorities for these jobs.

Scheduling involves two major activities: loading and setting priorities. It is often the primary focus of the dispatcher and the department supervisor. Scheduling provides information on what jobs are available, when they are to be started, when they are to be finished, and priorities.

Detailed sequencing, on the other hand, involves determining the sequence in which a manufacturing facility (e.g., a work center or a department) is to process the orders assigned to it so as to achieve certain objectives. This is a more detailed activity than scheduling. Detailed sequencing determines which order is to be processed next.

Whereas scheduling is done on a regular basis (e.g., once every shift, once every week), detailed sequencing is done whenever the manufacturing facility has completed one job and is ready to begin another. In many job shops, the involvement of the operator often makes scheduling an activity separate from detailed sequencing.

## TECHNIQUES USED IN THE DISPATCHING PROCESS

A large number of procedures employed within the job shop are potentially useful in the dispatching process. Of these procedures, some are useful in identifying the priority of a specific job found at a given work center or the sequence in which jobs should be processed, while others can be used to manage the flow of jobs to and from work centers. Of these procedures, the most commonly used are the following:

### Backward/Forward Scheduling

The PAC system uses two related sets of dates: the *order start date/order due date* and the *operation start dates/operation due dates*. The order due date identifies the time at which the order must have completed all of its operations and be available for use. The order start date is the time at which the order is to begin processing on the shop floor. These two dates, which are very important to the planning system, identify the starting and stopping points for the entire order. They also provide a crucial link between the planning system and PAC. The order due date used by the PAC system should be consistent with the order need date used by the planning system. If the planning system changes the order need date, the order due date should be changed to maintain consistency.

Between these dates falls the manufacturing lead time. For personnel on the shop floor, these two dates, while important, do not provide enough information. In the job shop, each order has to go through several operations. These operations may include not only processing but also material picking, inspection, and moving to and from stores. Personnel should know when to start and finish these various operations in order to meet the order due date. This requires a set of start dates and due dates for each operation contained in the routing. These operation start dates and due dates can be determined by the use of either *forward* or

---

**FIGURE 10** Relationship between Operation Start Dates and Operation Due Dates

---

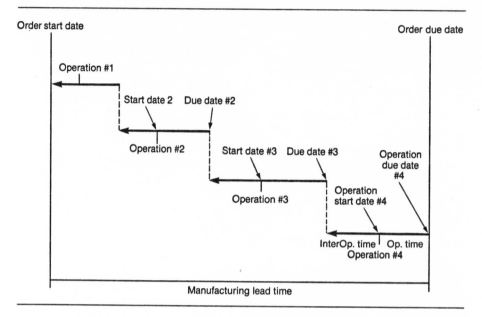

backward scheduling. The relationship between the operation start dates/due dates and the order start date/due date is shown in Figure 10.

For most PAC systems, backward scheduling is the preferred procedure. Backward scheduling begins with the order due date (identified by the planning system in the form of the order need date) at the *last* operation in the routing. The operation due date for the last operation must be the same as the order due date. From this date, backward scheduling works backward through the routing. It subtracts from the operation due date the time required by all the activities required at the work center (i.e., the operation lead time). These activities usually include the operation time (needed to arrive at the operation start time, i.e., the time at which the operation is to start—which should consider the lot size and setup times), the queue time (based on the standard queue time allowances—to identify when the order should be available at the work center), and the standard transit allowance (if applicable). After the operation lead time for the last operation has been determined, the operation due date for the next to the last operation can be identified. The procedure is repeated backward through all of the operations required by the order (as described in the routing). For each operation, backward scheduling has identified an operation due date, an operation start date, and an operation arrival date (when the order can be expected to arrive at the work center).

The backward scheduling procedure is illustrated in Figure 11. In this example, we are backward-scheduling an order for part #B43269. All times are converted into days (they could also be done easily in terms of percentage of a day). The order has a due date of 320 (using a numbered day scheduling calendar for scheduling shop operations). There is a standard allowance of one-day transit between actual processing operations (i.e., operations 20, 30, 40, 50, and 60). Based on this information, we can identify not only the order start date (day 287) but also the operation due dates for each of the eight operations identified on the routing.

Forward scheduling uses a logic similar to that of backward scheduling. Forward scheduling begins with the first operation in the routing and works forward to the last operation. Of the two procedures, backward scheduling is more common since most PAC systems begin with the order due date and schedule operations to meet this target.

The operation due dates and start dates calculated are used by the PAC system in at least two ways. First, orders waiting in queue can be sequenced based on either earliest operation due date or earliest operation start date. These dispatching rules are examined in greater detail in the discussion of dispatching/priority rules. Second, the operation start and due dates provide users with an easily understood method of judging the progress of orders. Orders that have not begun processing by their operation start date or have not been completed by their operation due date are behind schedule and are therefore sources of potential problems for the PAC system.

*A word on identifying dates on the shop floor.* How the backward scheduling logic represents the dates is very dependent on the scheduling calendar used by the manufacturing system. Two major types of scheduling or shop calendars are currently in

**FIGURE 11** Backward Scheduling Illustrated

Part #B43269

Routing/Scheduling Data

| Operation | Department | Machine | Description | Setup (hrs.) | Run (hrs.) | Days | Queue | Transit |
|---|---|---|---|---|---|---|---|---|
| 10 | 09 | | Issue material | | | 01 | | 01 |
| 20 | 32 | L034 | Rough turn | 1.5 | 0.030 | | 02 | 01 |
| 30 | 17 | H344 | Heat treat | | | 05 | 02 | 01 |
| 40 | 32 | L038 | Finish turn | 3.3 | 0.048 | | 02 | 01 |
| 50 | 12 | M200 | Mill face | 1.8 | 0.025 | | 02 | 01 |
| 60 | 12 | M260 | Mill slots | 0.6 | 0.010 | | 01 | |
| 95 | 11 | | Inspect | | | 03 | | |
| 99 | 40 | | Move stores | | | 01 | | |
| Totals | | | | 7.2 | 0.113 | 10 | 09 | 05 |

---

**FIGURE 11 (concluded)**

---

Operation Due Dates Identified
through Backward Scheduling

| Part #B43289 Order #5038 Due Date: 320 Order quantity: 300 | | | | |
|---|---|---|---|---|
| Operation | Hours | Days | Start | Operation Due Date |
| 10 | | 01 | 287 | 288 |
| 20 | 10.5 | 04 | 288 | 292 |
| 30 | | 07 | 293 | 300 |
| 40 | 17.7 | 05 | 301 | 306 |
| 50 | 9.3 | 04 | 307 | 312 |
| 60 | 3.6 | 02 | 313 | 315 |
| 95 | | 03 | 316 | 319 |
| 99 | | 01 | 319 | 320 |
| Totals | 41.1 | | | |

Note: The operation due dates and the start dates do not coincide due to the one-day transport time between operations.

use: the numbered-week calendar and the M-day (numbered-day) calendar [13, pp. 70–72]. The numbered-week calendar maintains the same week numbering scheme used by a formal planning system such as MRP (thus facilitating the coordination of these two systems). Within each week, each production day is identified. The result is typically a three-character identifier for each production day, in which the first two characters represent the production week and the third character represents the specific day in the production week. For example, 355 represents the fifth day of the 35th week. In contrast, the numbered-day calendar numbers only working days without referring to the production week. Depending on the type of scheduling calendar being used, the backward scheduling logic may have to make the appropriate adjustments to the dates. In the case of the numbered-week calendar, the logic must ensure that each of the identified operation dates falls in the appropriate production week.

### Input/Output Planning and Control

Strictly speaking, input/output planning and control is not a dispatching procedure. It is a short-term procedure for controlling capacity by monitoring the actual input and output rates, comparing these rates with planned input and output, and taking corrective actions whenever necessary. Input/output planning and control enables the user to:

Project capacity requirements into the future.
Develop a plan to level (smooth) these requirements.
Understand the relationship between input and output.

This procedure applies to the work center the logic and lessons found in the order review/release phase of production activity control. Planned backlogs at each of the various work centers are controlled by focusing on the rate at which orders are released to the work center and the rate at which work is cleared through the center (see Figure 12). Care is taken to ensure that the input is less than or equal to the output rate. Work in excess of the capacity of the work center is kept off the floor until the necessary capacity becomes available. The effective use of input/output planning and control can simplify the operation of such dispatching procedures as priority rules by reducing queues and controlling load variability. By reducing queues, input/output planning and control simplifies the dispatching decision. After all, it is easier to sequence 2 or 3 jobs than it is to sequence 10 or 15.

In controlling the release of work to the work center, input/output planning and control applies a principle first identified by Oliver Wight [16, pp. 9–31]. That is, over a given time period (e.g., day, shift, or week), never release more work to a work center than can be done at that work center in the same time period. If more work is available for release than the work center can handle, that excess work should be held off the floor (and the work center) and kept in production and inventory control. This principle is illustrated in Figure 12.

In short, input/output planning and control offers managers an important tool by which lead times can be effectively managed.

Input/output planning and control involves five elements [3, p. 140]:

**FIGURE 12** Basics of Input/Output Control Illustrated

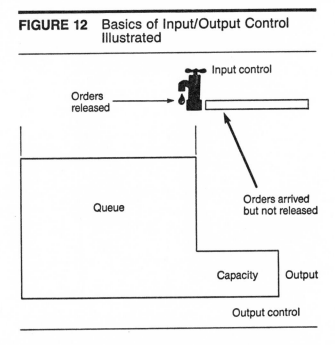

1. Setting the planned input to and output from work centers, usually for a short-range time period (e.g., a week).
2. Determining in advance the maximum deviation acceptable (i.e., differences between planned and actual) on both inputs and outputs.
3. Controlling the release of orders to production.
4. Measuring the actual inputs released to the work center and the actual outputs and comparing these with the expectations contained in the plan.
5. Analyzing for cause those variations that lie beyond the tolerances set in Step 2 and identifying and implementing the appropriate corrective action.

The application of input/output planning and control can be best illustrated by the example shown in Figure 13. Input/output planning and control consists of three major components: the input plan, the output plan, and the backlog analysis. In this example, the input and output plans are presented for a six-week period (weeks 18 to 23) for work center 123 and are current as of the end of week 22. It is the intent of management to maintain a

**FIGURE 13**  Input/Output Control Illustrated

Work center:  123

Backlog | Unreleased | 30 hours

Weeks

| | | 18 | 19 | 20 | 21 | 22 | 23 |
|---|---|---|---|---|---|---|---|
| **Input** | Planned input | 100 | 100 | 100 | 100 | 100 | 100 |
| | Actual input | 100 | 102 | 103 | 95 | 100 | |
| | Cumulative deviation | 0 | +2 | +5 | 0 | 0 | |
| **Output** | Planned output | 110 | 110 | 110 | 110 | 110 | 110 |
| | Actual output | 115 | 101 | 88 | 85 | 88 | |
| | Cumulative deviation | −5 | +4 | +26 | +51 | +73 | |
| | Actual backlog  50 | 35 | 36 | 51 | 61 | 73 | |

level input load of 100 hours and to maintain output at a level of 110 hours per week. The intent of these two plans is to reduce the released backlog by 10 hours per week. The actual backlog has grown from 50 hours at the beginning to 73 hours by the end of week 22. In addition, the planner has withheld 30 hours of work from the shop floor. In analyzing the input/output report contained in Figure 13, it can be seen that the problem lies primarily on the output side. Actual output has lagged behind planned output. If the work center is to realize the planned reduction in the backlog, it must produce at the planned output rate or be prepared to make up the shortages through overtime, subcontracting, alternative routings, a second shift, and so forth. In this case, there seems to be a persistent problem with output. It is now up to the department supervisor, working with the operator and the dispatcher, to identify the causes of this problem (e.g., a new operator, unsatisfactory machine maintenance) and to take the appropriate corrective actions.

Input/output planning and control offers several important advantages for the dispatching process. It provides:

1. A plan against which to judge performance.
2. A means for adjustment of the plan (on either the input or output side) on the basis of actual occurrences.
3. A method for controlling the release of work to a work center and for establishing rules governing the release of work to a work center (e.g., work can be released only to fill the void between the planned input and the planned output).
4. A method for clearly identifying the responsibilities of the upstream work centers (to maintain the planned rate of input) and of the various work centers (to maintain the planned rate of output).[1]

If the input/output report is to be used effectively as a control device, a tolerance is required. The tightness of this tolerance as well as the degree of control over the inputs and outputs is often related to the type of work center. Typically, the most

---

[1]Milwaukee APICS Chapter, *APICS Training Aid: Shop Floor Control* (Washington, D.C.: American Production and Inventory Control Society, 1973), p. 27.

tightly controlled work centers are gateway work centers and work centers that are bottlenecks.

In general, the effectiveness of input/output planning and control is related to the effectiveness of the capacity planning process. Input/output planning and control is most effective when adequate planned capacity is available on a period-to-period basis. When capacity availability is uncertain, input/output planning and control is no more than a short-term fire-fighting tool. It cannot compensate for poor capacity planning by the manufacturing planning system.

## Dispatching/Priority Rules

For every work center, the PAC should be able to rank the waiting orders in terms of urgency—from most urgent (highest priority) to least urgent (lowest priority). This ranking provides the operator with a recommended sequence in which to process the orders. Most often, the task of initially ranking orders is accomplished by means of a priority rule (also referred to as a dispatching rule). A priority rule can be defined as a set of steps for assigning priorities to orders waiting to be processed at a given work center [15, p. 8].

If there is one area in which there is an overabundance, it is in the area of dispatching rules. Past studies in scheduling, sequencing, and dispatching have identified over 100 priority rules. Among the more commonly used priority rules are the following:

1. *First Come, First Served (FCFS)*. Orders are processed in the same sequence in which they arrive at the work center. This rule is extremely simple to implement and use since it does not require a computer. All that has to be done is to record the time when orders arrive and to use this as the recommended sequence. Unfortunately, this rule ignores such important information as order due date, operation due date, processing time, and similarity of setup or processing. Generally, this is not a recommended priority rule. It can be used successfully only when the work center queue has been reduced to a few jobs. True just-in-time manufacturing systems use FCFS because they work with very small queues.

2. *Shortest Processing Time/Shortest Operation Time (SPT/ SOT)*. The order with the shortest processing time (i.e., setup

plus operating time) or the shortest operation time at the work center is the next one to be processed. This rule offers important advantages. It can maximize the number of jobs processed through a work center within a given time period. Its use generates the smallest average order lateness. Under conditions when order due dates are either infeasible or very suspect, SPT/SOT is the most appropriate rule to use. Like FCFS, however, SPT/SOT is not generally recommended. Its use can result in the infinite delay of orders requiring large amounts of processing time. Furthermore, in any system based on meeting due dates (such as MRP), the use of SPT/SOT conflicts with objectives of the overall system since this rule ignores any due date information. Generally, SPT/SOT is recommended only for PAC systems in which due dates are not useful criteria for dispatching. Order point systems are appropriate settings for SPT/SOT since the due dates generated by these systems are not based on the timing of the planning system's need (as they are in MRP) but are calculated on the basis of the order release date and the manufacturing lead time.

3. *Earliest Due Date (EDD)*. The order with the earliest due date is run next. In general, this rule is consistent with the operation of a due date–driven system such as MRP. Furthermore, EDD encourages the on-time delivery of orders. However, the EDD priority rule suffers from two major problems. First, to operate most effectively, EDD requires attainable order due dates. Due dates that are either tight or infeasible work poorly with this dispatching rule. Second, and more important, the EDD rule presents a distorted view of the urgency of the order, depending on whether the order is at the start of its operations or approaching completion. Because EDD ignores the remaining processing time when calculating priorities, orders just released to the shop tend to be given lower priorities (based on due dates alone) when compared to orders completing processing. These priorities may be biased because the orders just released may have their lead times completely taken up with processing. Priorities increase under EDD as the order is completed and nears its due date. In general, EDD is appropriate when orders tend to follow the same routing and when the remaining processing time does not constitute a critical component of the total manufacturing lead time.

4. *Slack Time Remaining (SLACK)*. Under this priority rule,

the order with the smallest slack is run next. Slack is defined as the difference between the current time and the order due date (after the remaining processing time has been subtracted). Like EDD, SLACK is appropriate for a due date–driven PAC system and is sensitive to the feasibility and tightness of order due dates. Unlike EDD, SLACK considers the amount of remaining processing time when calculating priorities. A major weakness of SLACK is that it ignores the number of remaining operations in the priority calculation.

5. *Slack Time per Remaining Operations (S/OPN)*. The priority of an order is determined by dividing the slack time (as calculated in SLACK) by the number of remaining operations. The order with the smallest ratio is processed next.

6. *Critical Ratio Rule (CRR)*. The critical ratio is defined as the order's slack divided by the remaining lead time (where the order's slack is the difference between the order due date and the current date). The order with the smallest ratio is processed next. The order's critical ratio indicates its urgency and status. An order with a critical ratio of less than 1 is behind schedule; a critical ratio greater than 1 indicates an order that is ahead of schedule, while a critical ratio of 1 indicates an order that is on schedule. Until recently, CRR was widely advocated as being the most appropriate dispatching rule for many due date–driven job shops. The major problem with CRR is that it states its priorities in the form of ratios. Priorities expressed in this way may not be meaningful to shop floor personnel.[2] Less and less use is being made of CRR.

7. *Queue Ratio (QR)*. The queue ratio is calculated as the remaining slack time divided by the remaining planned queue time. Orders with the smallest QRs are typically processed first.

8. *Operation Due Date/Operation Start Date (ODD/OSD)*. This priority rule first establishes the operation due date or start date using the backward/forward scheduling logic discussed earlier. The orders are then arranged in terms of smallest values. Increasingly, this rule is becoming the rule of choice for due date–driven systems. Like the other due date–based priority rules (EDD, SLACK, S/OPN, CRR, and QR), ODD/OSD is consistent with the operation of MRP systems. ODD/OSD also con-

---

[2]This aspect of CRR will be discussed in greater detail later in this section.

siders the effect of the remaining lead time components (processing time, setup time, move time, queue and wait time). Finally, and most important, ODD/OSD states the priorities in terms meaningful to most shop floor personnel. Most shop floor personnel can readily compare the operation due date with the current date to see whether the order is on schedule. Firms such as Twin Disc of Racine, Wisconsin, long considered to be a classic user of CRR, have switched to an ODD dispatching rule for this reason.

The operation of these eight priority rules is illustrated and compared in Figure 14.

As has been noted, the above list is not exhaustive.[3] Seven of the rules listed are time-based. They focus on such criteria as meeting due dates and minimizing order lateness. However, other criteria may be considered in developing a priority rule. These criteria include minimizing setup times, maximizing the dollar volume produced by the shop, maximizing the profit generated by the shop, and reducing machine or worker idle time.

When selecting and using priority rules, the following factors should always be borne in mind:

1. *The priority rules used to sequence overdue orders can be different from the priority rules used to sequence other orders.* For overdue orders, the dispatcher can choose, for example, to:

Run those orders first that have the greatest total of days behind schedule plus manufacturing lead time remaining.

Run those orders first that have the greatest total of days behind schedule plus processing time remaining [3, p. 392].

2. *Priority rules should be simple to use.* If a priority rule is to be used effectively, the user must be able to learn quickly how it operates. A good rule of thumb is that if it takes more than five minutes to explain the rule, the rule is very likely not to be used.

3. *Priority rules should be transparent and valid.* The logic behind a priority rule should be clear to the users so that they can readily understand the advantages of using it.

---

[3]For a more detailed discussion of such dispatching rules and procedures as Johnson's algorithm, the reader is directed to D. W. Fogarty and T. R. Hoffmann, *Production and Inventory Management* (Cincinnati: South-Western Publishing, 1983), appendix F ("Sequencing"), pp. 599–603.

---

**FIGURE 14** Operation of Priority Rules Illustrated

---

Shop order: 122456MH

| | |
|---|---|
| Number of pieces in order: | 50 |
| Order due date: | 215 |
| Current date: | 195 |
| Current status: | Released |
| Current location: | Operation 30 (Work Center 104) |
| Location in queue (based on arrival): | 3rd |

*Processing information for 122456MH:*

| Operation Number | Setup + Run | Queue | Total | Status |
|---|---|---|---|---|
| 10 | 2.35 | 1.0 | 3.35 | Complete |
| 20 | 4.50 | 3.0 | 7.50 | Complete |
| 30 | 3.50 | 3.0 | 6.50 | Just arrived |
| 40 | 2.50 | 2.0 | 4.50 | |
| 50 | 1.00 | 1.0 | 2.00 | |

Note: All times in dates; transit time between operations: 0.0 days.

*Priority of 122456MH using:*

FCFS:
   3rd   (based on time of arrival)

SPT:
   3.5   (positioned ahead of orders with (setup + run) times more than 3.5 and behind orders with smaller times)

EDD:
   215   (its order due date)

SLACK:

   Slack = Order due date − Current time − Remaining (Run + Setup) time − Remaining transit time − Remaining queue time

   = 215 − 195 − 7.0 − 0.0 − 6.0

   = 7

S/OPN:

   = Slack/Remaining operations

   = 7/3

   = 2.33

---

**FIGURE 14** *(concluded)*

---

CRR:

$$= \frac{\text{Order due date} - \text{Current time}}{\text{Lead time remaining}}$$
$$= (215 - 195)/13$$
$$= 20/13$$
$$= 1.54 \text{ (indicates that the order is ahead of schedule)}$$

QR:

$$= \frac{\text{Slack remaining in operation}}{\text{Planned queue time in current operation}}$$
$$= \frac{(20 - 4.5 - 2.0) - 3.5}{3.0}$$
$$= 3.33$$

ODD:

First establish operation dates for:

| | |
|---|---|
| Operation 5: | 215 |
| | − 2.0 |
| Operation 4: | 213 |
| | − 4.5 |
| Operation 3: | 208.5* |

---

*4. Priority rules should generate meaningful priorities.* A priority rule should generate priorities that can be readily interpreted. In many job shops, it is natural for dispatchers, department supervisors, and operators to think in terms of either operation start dates or operation due dates. As a result, rules such as ODD and OSD are inherently attractive to many PAC personnel. CRR suffers from a major shortcoming—its priorities are stated in terms of fractions that are not readily understandable.

*5. The priority rule must be consistent with the operation and objectives of the planning system.* The priority rule should ensure that the priorities used on the shop floor reflect those found in the planning system. MRP, for example, is a due date–driven system—it identifies order due dates that must be met to maintain the overall feasibility of the generated plans. In such an environment, rules such as SPT and FCFS should not be used since they are inconsistent with the due date orientation of MRP.

Using such rules would convey the "wrong" message to those working on the shop floor. The use of a rule such as SPT might imply that processing the largest number of orders through a work center is more important than meeting due dates—a position in direct conflict with the objectives of MRP.

6. *A priority rule is never a substitute for capacity planning.* A priority rule works best if there is enough capacity to process the orders in the work center. A priority rule should not be used to decide how to ration out an inadequate amount of capacity. Such a situation leads to frustration for everyone.

7. *The priorities generated by any priority rule should be regarded as recommendations.* Priority rules identify order sequences that satisfy certain predetermined criteria (e.g., meeting order due dates). However, no priority rule can consider all of the factors that affect the ultimate sequence. As pointed out previously, this sequence should be assigned to the operator—a person who should be aware of these factors. The priority rules provide inputs alone. Only under conditions of high-capacity utilization (85–90 percent and over) should the sequences generated by the dispatching rules be strictly followed. Under such conditions, rearranging orders involves delaying one or more jobs while others are brought forward. Because there is no slack in the form of excess capacity, these delayed jobs will fall behind schedule. The operator has now created a problem for the PAC system—that of bringing these delayed orders back on schedule.

## Gantt Charts

Developed by H. L. Gantt in 1917, the Gantt chart is one of the oldest planning and scheduling tools available to production activity control. Also called a "bar graph," the Gantt chart is simply a way of *graphically* showing:

The scheduling of jobs across operations and the monitoring of their progress.

The loading of machine centers and the evaluation of such loading in light of available capacity.

Project scheduling (used in conjunction with CPM and PERT).

In each of these three tasks, the Gantt chart provides the user with a quick and visual method for identifying the actual status and comparing it with the anticipated status.

An example of a Gantt chart for the scheduling of a job across operations is found in Figure 15. In this example, the order, #12345, has six operations, displayed in the columns, and is expected to take six weeks to complete. The project is currently in week 4, as indicated by the caret (V). The light horizontal lines indicate the planned lead time for each operation in the bill of routing, while the heavy horizontal lines indicate actual progress. The start and due dates for each of the operations can be set using either backward or forward scheduling. More informational detail can be added to the Gantt chart by using the set of available Gantt chart symbols.[4]

By comparing the planned with the actual progress of the order, the user can determine whether the order is on schedule and, if there are problems, where the problems are. In this example, we can see that the third operation has been started late and has not yet been completed. Management now knows where corrective action must be taken if the order due date is to be met.

In using the Gantt chart for machine loading, the form taken by the chart is modified. The rows now represent the various machine centers. For each machine center, the columns represent the scheduling periods (weeks or months). An example of the use of a Gantt chart for machine loading is found in Figure 16. In this example, the capacity loadings are represented in two forms for each machine. The light line represents the projected load by week, while the heavy line represents the accumulated backlog of work. Overloaded and underloaded machines can be easily identified using this form of the Gantt chart.

Gantt charts are widely used (though their use is declining). They are simple to use and provide a useful method of representing information. Changes to the schedule (or loads) and current progress can be easily incorporated into them. Finally, Gantt charts can be done on a wide variety of mediums, ranging from a

---

[4]A detailed discussion of these symbols and the Gantt chart procedure can be found in J. H. Greene, *Production and Inventory Control* (Homewood, Ill.: Richard D. Irwin, 1974), pp. 346–49.

**FIGURE 15** An Example of the Gantt Chart Procedure

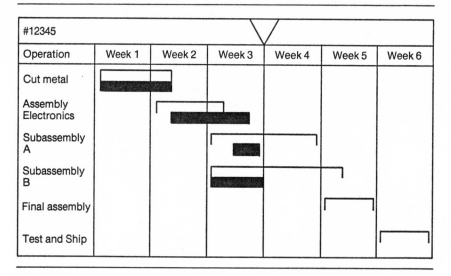

**FIGURE 16** Gantt Chart for Machine Loading

| Department 104 | | For production weeks 26-31 | | | | | |
|---|---|---|---|---|---|---|---|
| Machine | Mach No. | 26 | 27 | 28 | 29 | 30 | 31 |
| Lathe 4 | 123 | | | | | | |
| Lathe 5 | 124 | | | | | | |
| Gisholt 2 | 331 | | | | | | |
| Gisholt 3 | 332 | | | | | | |
| W&S 2 | 442 | | | | | | |
| W&S 3 | 443 | | | | | | |
| Mill 8 | 668 | | | | | | |

piece of ruled paper with the proper scale to mechanical devices such as the Produc-trol Board and the Sched-U-Graph.

## Other Procedures

There are numerous other dispatching procedures that are potentially useful. Since it is not possible to discuss all of these procedures, we shall identify only some of the more noteworthy of these procedures, briefly describe their most important features, and, where possible, provide the reader with one or more recommended readings.

**Short-Interval Scheduling.** This is a method of scheduling in which a planned quantity of work is assigned to a work center to be completed in a specific period of time (usually 60 minutes or less). The work is evaluated frequently to ensure that it has been completed within the time specified. Short-interval scheduling is based on the notion that efficiency will always be improved if the firm can control the interval on an ongoing basis. More information on this scheduling procedure can be found in [4, pp. 386–87].

**Simulation.** Simulation is the process of developing and using a computer-based model of a real system (i.e., a department, a work center, or the entire job shop) in order to evaluate alternative policies or solutions. These policies can consist of different dispatching rules (e.g., ODD versus SPT) or dispatching procedures (e.g., input/output planning and control). They can also consist of different order sequences or workloads. The major advantage of simulation is that it allows for "What if?" experimentation. Alternative policies are first implemented in the computer simulation, and their effects are identified and compared. Based on these experiments, the user can not only identify the most appropriate policy but can also determine in advance what effects that policy will have on the operation of the system over time. Simulations of job shops, developed for the purposes of dispatching by such firms as Hughes, have been in use since the 1950s and 1960s. Currently, this procedure, while not widely used, is being used more frequently—a situation due in part to the availability of cheaper computer power and the advantage of such production systems as flexible manufacturing systems (FMS).[5]

**Line of Balance Technique.** This method of planning and scheduling production is suitable for job shops consisting of complex assemblies. The line of balance technique consists of three charts (the planning chart, the objective chart, and the progress chart) that, used together, tell users how they are doing with respect to the plan and help users identify potential problem areas. This technique is described in greater detail in [4, pp. 372–74].

Other dispatching procedures, such as queueing theory, branch and bound, and dynamic programming, are beyond the scope of this book. References for these procedures can be found in [11, appendixes A and D].

## REQUIREMENTS FOR EFFECTIVE DISPATCHING

For the dispatching process to be effective, certain requirements must be in place. Some of these requirements have already been discussed, but the points made bear repeating. The most important of these requirements are:

1. *Feasible and credible order due dates.* The order due dates given to shop floor personnel must be attainable (feasible). There must be adequate capacity, material and tooling with which to meet the due dates without having to resort to expediting on a routine basis. The order due dates must always reflect the timing of actual needs.

2. *Communication of the recommended priorities by a dispatch list that provides the user with feasible priorities and access to information concerning incoming orders, the status of downstream work centers, and the status of orders assigned to the work center.* Priorities should be communicated by means of a

---

[5]FMS presents the PAC system with a very interdependent system. Dispatching decisions taken at one machine will have important implications for the operation of downstream work centers. Simulation is required to help the user identify these effects in advance. This aspect of FMS and simulation is discussed in Melnyk et al., *Shop Floor Control* (Homewood, Ill.: Dow Jones-Irwin, 1985), pp. 93–100.

dispatch list. The dispatch list should identify all of the orders currently in queue, and it should rank these jobs in order of decreasing priority (the most urgent job should be identified first). Figure 17 provides an example of an actual dispatch list.

The priorities reported in the dispatch list should be updated on a regular basis (at least once a day or once a shift). Frequent updating is necessary to maintain the validity of the priorities and the effectiveness of the dispatch list.

The dispatch list should also provide shop floor personnel with access (either directly on the dispatch list or by means of associated reports) to the following information:

- *Nature of Orders Scheduled.* Not all orders are the same. Some orders are for customers, while others are needed to replenish stock. The nature of the demand for the orders should be clearly indicated. If there is ever conflict in priorities, customer orders should always be given preference over orders for inventory replenishment.

- *Capacity Available and Capacity Required.* The user should be aware of the number of standard hours of capacity available from the work center, the number of days of production available, and the number of standard hours of work assigned to the work center for the given week. This information provides the user with an indication of the amount of flexibility (as measured in terms of excess or uncommitted capacity) available for the rearrangement of orders.

- *Work Center Look Ahead/Work Center Look Back.* The people involved in the dispatching process should have complete visibility over the shop load at a given work center. This visibility should cover upstream and downstream loads as well as the load at the work center. The information provided by this visibility is crucial in helping the user better manage the flow of work through a given work center.

    Using the look ahead/look back information, the user can better level shop load by work center. For example, jobs going to congested upstream work centers can be delayed in favor of those proceeding to relatively idle centers. The user can also identify orders that can be

# FIGURE 17 An Actual Dispatch List

DATE PRINTED 01/24/85  
SHOP CALENDAR DAY NUMBER 951  

JOB @5730F04 REPORT NUMBER 5732A  
WORK CENTER DAILY QUEUE LIST  

WORK CENTER 126-0930            DESCRIPTION CINCINNATI MTX

| DAYS E/L | SWAN | ---PART NUMBER---- | | DESCRIPTION | LOC | DUE DTE | SCHEDULED-THIS-W/C- OPER | ST | -S/U | --RUN- | --COMING-FROM--- OPER | -W/C--- | ST | -HRS- AWAY | -LAST-MOVE-REPORTED- OPER | -W/C--- | --QTY- | -ORDER- --QTY- |
|---|---|---|---|---|---|---|---|---|---|---|---|---|---|---|---|---|---|---|
| 13- | 145201A | A28784 | 003 | FRAME | ONC | 999 | 0070 | 40 | 7.5 | 3.1 | | | COMPLETED | | 0070 | 126-0343 | 24 | 24 |
| 7 | 141358A | A28784 | 003 | FRAME | ONC | 020 | 0140 | 30 | 1.8 | 24.6 | | | SSET- 6.3 SRUN- | 25.4 | 0070 | 126-0343 | 24 | 24 |
| 38 | 149823A | A28784 | 003 | FRAME | ONC | 060 | 0110 | 30 | -2.2 | 3.3 | | | SSET- 7.3 SRUN- | 25.6 | 0070 | 126-0343 | 24 | 24 |
| 13- | 145201A | A28784 | 003 | FRAME | ONC | 999 | 0140 | 20 | 6.3 | 25.4 | | | AVAILABLE | | 0070 | 126-0343 | 24 | 24 |
| 16 | 149815A | A28784 | 003 | FRAME | ONC | 040 | 0110 | 20 | 7.3 | 25.6 | | | AVAILABLE | | 0070 | 126-0343 | 24 | 24 |
| 30 | 144089A | A28764 | 003 | FRAME | ONC | 040 | 0140 | 20 | 6.3 | 23.3 | | | AVAILABLE | | 0070 | 126-0343 | 22 | 22 |
| 52 | 126797A | A22391 | 001 | PROFILE | ONC | 010 | 0120 | 20 | 3.0 | 14.0 | | | AVAILABLE | | 0120 | 126-0343 | 24 | 24 |
| 52 | 138727A | A22391 | 001 | PROFILE | ONC | 010 | 0120 | 20 | 3.0 | 14.0 | | | AVAILABLE | | 0120 | 126-0343 | 24 | 24 |
| 18 | 157677A | A28784 | 003 | FRAME | P15 | 060 | 0070 | 10 | 7.5 | 34.2 | 0060 | 123-0250 | 20 | 12 | 0040 | 123-0210 | 24 | 24 |

WORK CENTER 126-0930    CAPACITY= 58    CRIT Q HRS= 45    TTL LOAD HRS= 194    CRIT Q DAYS= 0.8    TTL Q DAYS= 3.4

**FIGURE 17** *(concluded)*

WORK CENTER DAILY QUEUE LIST

Legend

| | |
|---|---|
| Days Er/La | - Priority Number (Slack Time) |
| SWAN | - Work Order Number (Shop Work Authorization Number) |
| Part Number | - Self Explanatory |
| Description | - Self Explanatory |
| Loc | - Physical Location of Work Order |
| Due Dte | - Due Date |
| Scheduled-This-W/C | - Information on Operations to Be Performed in This Work Center |
| Oper | - Operation Number of Operation Being Performed or Due to Be Performed in This Work Center |
| St | - Status Code |
| |      50 - Operation Complete |
| |      40 - Operation Complete |
| |      30 - Operation Started |
| |      20 - Operation Available to Be Started |
| |      10 - Operation Scheduled Point Not Available |
| Su | - Standard Setup Hours (completed and started operations have actual hours subtracted from total setup hours) |
| Run | - Standard Run Hours (completed and started operations have actual hours subtracted from total run hours) |
| Coming-From | - Information on Operations Just prior to the Scheduled Operation |
| Oper | - Previous Operation Number (completed operations show total standard setup and run hours, available operations show as available) |
| W/C | - Previous Work Center |
| Hrs Away | - Total Standard Hours That Have to Be Completed before Work Order Arrives at This Work Center |
| Last-Move-Reported | - Information from Last Move Ticket Entered |
| Oper | - Operation Number Moved to |
| W/C | - Work Center Moved to |
| Qty | - Quantity Moved |
| Order Qty | - Start Quantity of Work Order |
| Wait Days | - Number of Days the Job Has Been Inactive |
| | |
| Total Line | |
| Capacity | - Daily Demonstrated Capacity |
| Crit Q Hrs | - Total Standard Hours Remaining and Available of Late Jobs |
| Ttl Load Hrs | - Total Standard Hours Remaining and Available of All Jobs |
| Crit Q Days | - Critical Queue Hours/Capacity |
| Ttl Q Days | - Total Load Hours Capacity |

pulled forward (e.g., to take advantage of order similarities). Finally, this information provides warning. Hot jobs can be identified in advance so that the work center is prepared to receive them.

- *A Clear Understanding of the Major Dispatching Criteria.* If personnel are to be effectively involved in the dispatching process, they must understand what the key objectives of dispatching are. They must be provided with two or three clearly stated key objectives. For example, in many effective PAC systems (such as those found in the Vollrath Corporation, Steelcase, Inc., and Twin Disc Corporation), all shop personnel are continually made aware of the importance of meeting the schedule. They are encouraged to improve efficiency by taking advantage of similarities in processes, components, or setups only as long as they can assure the dispatcher and management that these improvements in efficiency will not come at the expense of the schedule.

- *Accountability.* All persons involved in the dispatching process should be held accountable for their actions. Dispatchers should be held accountable for completing the work assigned to them in a timely fashion, and operators should be held accountable for clearing the work assigned to them by the due dates. Accountability helps ensure that objectives are met. It is the complement of the freedom that the dispatching process grants shop floor personnel. That is, operators, supervisors, and dispatchers "own" the work. They are free to rearrange it as long as they recognize that they will be evaluated on the basis of their actions.

## DISPATCHING CONSIDERATIONS AT THE VARIOUS WORK CENTERS

The typical job shop consists of a number of work centers. Not all of these work centers are equal, nor should they all conform to the same standards or the same tolerances. The work centers in a job shop can be broken down into three groups—each with its special considerations. These three groups are:

Gateway work centers.
Downstream work centers.
Final work centers.

## Gateway Work Centers

As their name implies, gateway work centers are work centers through which orders enter the job shop and begin processing. These work centers are critical to the operation of the entire job shop. How work is managed at them influences the operation of all downstream work centers. Sporadic, uneven loads at the gateway work centers may mean even more sporadic and more uneven loads at the downstream work centers. Consequently, effective dispatching at the gateway work centers requires:

1. *Tight Control of Inputs.* The amount of work released to gateway work centers must be controlled so that it matches capacity availability and so that it is level from period to period. Queues at gateway work centers should be small.

2. *Tight Tolerances.* Since any problems felt at gateway work centers will be felt downstream, problems on either the input or output side must not be allowed to develop. Tight tolerances force the user to monitor closely operations at these centers and to investigate any deviations.

3. *Close Cooperation with the Order Review/Release Stage of PAC.* Because the gateway work center is the first center to be loaded by newly released work, personnel from the order review/ release stage may be involved in the processing of dispatching work. For example, these personnel may delay the release of orders going to congested gateway work centers.

In short, the management of gateway work centers sets the tone for the rest of the job shop. Effective dispatching to the gateway work centers facilitates the effective management of the other work centers; ineffective dispatching to these centers increases the difficulties faced by the other centers.

## Downstream Work Centers

The downstream work centers face the problem of "interdependence." Their load is affected by the output of preceding work centers; their output affects the load of succeeding work centers. Therefore, effective dispatching to such work centers requires monitoring loads not only at the given work center but also at the preceding and succeeding work centers. The succeeding work centers are monitored in order to identify those that are currently congested. Such centers should be avoided, and the priorities of jobs going to uncongested work centers should be advanced.[6] In other words, the dispatching process at the downstream work centers should "push" the "right" mix of processed orders.

In addition, the downstream work center should "pull" forward orders from preceding work centers. When faced by excess or unused capacity, the operator may work with operators from other downstream work centers in adjusting priorities at these centers in order to provide needed work.

In short, effective dispatching at the downstream work centers involves coordination and cooperation among work centers.

## Final Work Centers

As pointed out in [3, p. 401], management of the final work centers is crucial to the overall performance of the shop because the outputs of these work centers affect such areas as shipments, billings, accounts receivable, and cash flow. Effective dispatching at final work centers is concerned with two tasks: (1) coordination of production with either the master production schedule (MPS) or the final assembly schedule (FAS) and (2) control over the inputs to the final work centers. The first task is required to ensure that the final work center produces what is actually required by the planning system. The second task ensures that the final work center has the "right" items at the "right" time and in the "right" quantity so that it can complete the desired output on time. This second task is the primary focus of dispatching at final work centers.

---

[6]One dispatching technique which incorporates the status of succeeding work centers in determining order priorities has been suggested in R. J. Schonberger, "Clearest-Road-Ahead Priorities for Shop Floor Control: Moderating Infinite-Capacity-Loading Unevenness," *Production and Inventory Management* 20, no. 2 (1979), pp. 17–27.

## STEPS IN THE DISPATCHING PROCESS

The various dispatching procedures and factors discussed in the preceding sections, when put together, form major elements of the dispatching process. This process consists of the following major steps:

1. *Establish the dispatching interval.* The first step and one that should be taken during the development of the dispatching process is to identify the dispatching interval. The dispatching interval is the time interval between the generation of new dispatch lists by the dispatcher and their implementation. The interval can vary from a week to minutes. Orders are most frequently dispatched to work centers on either a weekly basis or a shift basis. The interval selected should reflect the best trade-off between accuracy of results and computer processing time. The shorter the interval, the more accurate the priorities given to and used in the shop. The longer the interval between the generation of new dispatch lists, the less the computer processing time incurred.

2. *Identify the jobs that are to be processed during the following time period.* Typically, work centers are given enough orders to carry them through a week of production. These orders can be identified in one of four ways:

   a. The existing backlog (i.e., orders issued to the work center in the past but not yet completed).
   b. Orders released by the planning system to the work center (most appropriate in the case of gateway work centers).
   c. Orders completed by preceding work centers and ready for processing by the given work center.
   d. Orders identified by the PAC system as having either an operation start date or an operation due date falling in the given week.

These four sources form the entire pool of potential orders that can be dispatched by the dispatcher.

3. *Review and evaluate the potential orders.* Not all of the orders identified in the second step should be considered when determining which orders are to be dispatched at a given work center. Orders should be excluded (i.e., not released to the work center) for the following reasons:

a. They have not cleared their previous operation.
b. A change in customer requirements, reflected in the order due date, has reduced the urgency of need for the job.
c. A job has completed its previous operations early and has a great deal of slack present.
d. The order is on schedule, but one or more of the cocomponents required by the parent order has experienced delays.
e. The job is available for processing, but the tooling required by the job is currently not available.

Of the five reasons, the second and fourth are noteworthy because they involve dependent priorities. The second reason involves vertical dependency, while the fourth reason involves horizontal dependency.[7] All potential orders should be regularly reviewed and evaluated by the dispatcher because that person is responsible for the work scheduled at the work centers under his control.

4. *Identify the amount of capacity available.* Next, the dispatcher, with the assistance of the department supervisor (if appropriate), must determine the amount of capacity available. This capacity should set the limit to the amount of work that can be scheduled in any work center within the dispatching interval. The amount of capacity available should be stated in terms of such measures as standard hours, load factor,[8] and effective daily capacity. Under certain conditions, the dispatcher may base his capacity evaluation on the amount of capacity available during the last dispatching interval (i.e., never load any more work than was processed in the last interval).

5. *Prioritize the orders to be released.* After excluding jobs, the dispatcher should rank the remaining orders. This ranking should be generated by the application of the appropriate dispatching procedure (e.g., the ODD priority rule). It forms the basis of the dispatch list.

6. *Load the work center.* Next, the dispatcher, working with

---

[7]The concept of dependent priorities is discussed in greater detail in J. A. Orlicky, *Material Requirements Planning* (New York: McGraw-Hill, 1975), pp. 146–50.

[8]The load factor can be defined as a ratio equal to the number of actual hours required to clear one standard hour of work.

the department supervisor (if applicable), should identify the specific work centers to which the orders are to be dispatched. The capabilities of the work center should be matched to the characteristics of the orders to be processed. The dispatcher should never dispatch more work to a center than the center has capacity to handle.

7. *Identify the actual sequence of orders.* Depending on conditions, the actual sequence can be determined by the dispatcher and communicated to the operator by means of the dispatch list. This situation can occur under conditions of high-capacity utilization. Alternatively, the actual sequence can be identified by the operator. In this case, the priorities contained in the dispatch list are only inputs. The operator is free to rearrange the sequence to improve efficiency.

8. *Identify any important special conditions, and adjust the priorities to reflect these conditions.* The ultimate priorities assigned to orders should reflect such important considerations as [6, p. 76]:

   *a.* Operation grouping: grouping jobs together to take advantage of similarities in processing, setups or parts.
   *b.* Time-critical operations: where a subsequent operation has to be performed during a certain time of the previous operation.
   *c.* Related facilities: where two or more facilities must be available to perform the operation.
   *d.* Overlapped and split operations.
   *e.* Alternative operations and routing: considering the use of other work centers (usually at a cost such as increased setup time) to prevent jobs from being delayed.
   *f.* Split lot sizes.
   *g.* Operations done out of sequence.

9. *Revise priorities.* Priorities should be revised on a timely basis.

As can be seen from this discussion, the process for dispatching orders is a complex one. It is also one that frequently requires cooperation among the dispatcher, the department supervisor, and the machine operator. In reviewing this process, certain "lessons" should be noted:

- The dispatcher and the planning system should be responsible for the feasibility of the schedules released to the operator; the operator should use his detailed knowledge of the product and process to improve efficiency.
- The flexibility to rearrange orders is a function of the amount of excess capacity available.
- Dispatching is not synonymous with the use of a priority rule.
- Detailed load leveling of the shop should be done by shop floor personnel.

## SCHEDULING OF PREVENTIVE MAINTENANCE

The act of production is both a constructive and destructive process. Production is necessary to create output. Each hour of production, however, subjects machinery and tools to varying degrees of wear and tear. If nothing is done, these resources will become unable to provide the functions for which they were acquired. Some form of maintenance program is therefore necessary. There are basically two types of maintenance programs:

1. *Breakdown Maintenance:* emergency maintenance, including diagnosis of the problem and repair of the machine, facility, or tooling, only after a malfunction has occurred [5, p. 13].
2. *Preventive Maintenance:* maintenance that is done at regular intervals. Included in preventive maintenance are such operations as lubrication and inspection and such major jobs as the overhaul of a press [5, p. 13]. Unlike breakdown maintenance, preventive maintenance describes any maintenance that is not triggered by the breakdown of the machine, facility, or tooling.

Both types of maintenance programs should be under the control of the PAC system because they require the detailed allocation of personnel, material, tooling, and machinery. The scheduling of maintenance requires answering almost the same questions that the PAC personnel must answer when scheduling orders—questions regarding the types of resources to be used, the quantity of resources, the timing of the assignment, and the urgency of the task.

Breakdown maintenance is relatively straightforward. When a

machine or tooling breaks down, processing is stopped and the problem corrected. At the moment the breakdown occurs, maintenance receives the highest priority. This type of maintenance program is undesirable for several reasons. Breakdowns tend to occur at the most inconvenient times. Because they occur randomly, they become a source of uncertainty and lead time variability. The planning system can respond to this variability and uncertainty either by increasing the planned lead time or by carrying more safety stock. Both of these actions can be extremely costly and can adversely affect the firm's ability to compete. As a general rule, breakdown maintenance should be avoided.

Preventive maintenance, at first glance, may seem to involve the unproductive use of shop floor resources in that it produces no additional units of output. Preventive maintenance does reduce the availability of resources in the short run. In return, however, it improves the availability of those resources in the long run.

Preventive maintenance can be done either "in-process" or "out-of-process." In-process preventive maintenance should have no impact on capacity since no downtime is involved. It is maintenance that is normally performed:

Daily (e.g., oiling machines, cleaning equipment).
Weekly (e.g., electrically monitoring equipment).
Monthly (e.g., measuring table movements within tolerance).

In-process maintenance does not involve making the machine or tool unavailable for use by other shop orders. The operator is typically responsible for undertaking the actions required by this form of maintenance. In contrast, out-of-process maintenance has an impact on the capacity of the shop because it requires that a resource be turned over to maintenance. During this time, the resource cannot be used by any job.

Out-of-process maintenance requires the dispatching of a *work order.* A work order is an authorization for maintenance work to be done on a resource. It is similar to a shop order in that:

A lead time is involved.
A due date for the work order must be set.
The work order is a source of information (identifying labor

standards, interruption codes, type of labor required, and priority).

Because the work order results in a loss of capacity, it should be planned in advance. In addition, alternative action plans should be in place so that the disruptive impact on capacity introduced by the work order is kept to a minimum.

## Events Triggering the Issuance of a Work Order

The need for out-of-process maintenance can be indicated by two major types of events:

1. The end of the preventive maintenance interval has been reached.
2. Conditions indicating the need for preventive maintenance have been identified.

The first type of event can be best described as involving *planned* preventive maintenance. A preventive maintenance interval has been established previously. This interval, which can be stated in terms of the number of hours of operations, the number of pieces produced, or the number of strokes, indicates the amount of time that the resource on average can be expected to function without problems. When the end of this interval has been reached, preventive maintenance should be scheduled to maintain the effectiveness of the resource. The interval can be derived in several ways. It can be based on the manufacturer's guidelines; it can be derived by plant engineering; or it can be identified statistically.[9] The computer system can be used to monitor the interval and to identify when planned preventive maintenance is required.

In contrast, the second type of event is more accurately described as *unplanned* preventive maintenance. This event is frequently flagged by the occurrence of one or more of the following signals:

---

[9]The procedures for deriving the preventive maintenance interval are discussed in greater detail in IBM, *Communications Oriented Production Information and Control System,* vol. 6, chap. 6 (Plant Maintenance) (White Plains, N.Y.: IBM Corporation, Technical Publications, 1972), pp. 11–16.

An increase in scrap rate over a period of time.
An increase in setup time.
An increase in downtime.
A decrease in machine output.
Wide deviations from quality tolerances.

These signals indicate that the machine or tooling needs maintenance.

## Staffing

The effective scheduling of a work order cannot be done by the PAC system alone. It is a joint PAC, plant, and maintenance decision. The actual responsibility for reviewing and releasing work orders is given to the dispatcher in many systems.

## Steps in Dispatching a Work Order

The scheduling of out-of-process maintenance must be done in line with priority and capacity information. The work order should not be issued to the shop at a time when it would deprive certain high-priority orders of needed capacity or when the shop is working under short-term conditions of high-capacity utilization. In other words, the dispatcher should identify in advance the impact of the work order on the operation of the shop floor.

When the work order is issued, it should be given a priority and a due date (i.e., time of completion). For example, the preventive maintenance may be allowed to take place only after the jobs currently in queue have been completed. Alternatively, the work order may be placed at the head of the queue. The shop should be informed that the tool or work center will be undergoing preventive maintenance. This information can be used to adjust order priorities or to take advantage of alternative routings. For example, jobs proceeding to the work center scheduled for preventive maintenance may have their priorities reduced.

When the resource is undergoing preventive maintenance, capacity should be adjusted to reflect the resulting reduction.

In the case of an unplanned out-of-process maintenance, the machine may have to be taken out of service. The need to take the machine out of service should be reviewed by the dispatcher. In such instances, machine constraints should be identified and an action plan should be in place prior to the occurrence of the emergency situation.

As soon as possible after maintenance has been completed on the machine or tooling, the shop floor should be made aware of its availability.

## Other Considerations

In addition to the steps described in this section, the following factors should be borne in mind when scheduling preventive maintenance:

- MRP can and should be used to control maintenance and electrical inventories. The use of MRP will allow for effective management of this large company asset.
- Multilocation policies for multiple-plant access and transfer of maintenance inventories should be in place. In practice, such procedures have turned out to be highly cost effective.
- Action plans (i.e., methods of compensating for lost capacity due to maintenance) should be in place from the outset.
- Work orders should be routinely evaluated and reviewed for efficiency and timeliness of completion just as any other shop orders are.

## Dispatching of Preventive Maintenance— Summary Comments

Many PAC systems currently do not have any formal procedure for dispatching work orders in place. Preventive maintenance is often neglected as dispatchers and department supervisors try to meet production objectives. This situation is now becoming less acceptable. With the increased emphasis on reduced lead times and less variability in lead times and with the greater acceptance of just-in-time manufacturing practices and principles, preventive maintenance is now becoming a necessity of manufacturing life.

## SCHEDULING OF SCRAP, SALVAGE, AND REWORK

Most PAC systems have in place procedures for controlling the dispatching of shop orders; fewer PAC systems have procedures for the dispatching of rework and salvage. Salvage and rework arise whenever the specifications of the shop order cannot be satisfied (either in whole or in part).[10] At this point, a decision must be made on how to handle the problems. Whenever it is decided to rework the order by adding extra (rework) steps or to complete the order as salvage (either item or component), a formal dispatching procedure must be used. Without such a procedure, rework and salvage become "lost" orders to the PAC system. They are processed only when time is available (i.e., makework jobs) or when someone remembers that the need for some currently shorted (and critical) components can be filled from the shop floor by drawing on an order that is now salvage. Shop performance becomes difficult to evaluate and shop orders undergoing salvage or rework become difficult to track.

### Conditions Triggering Salvage and Rework

All rework and salvage must begin with a shop order that fails to meet a set of product specifications (either in whole or in part). The factors generating these out-of-tolerance conditions should be identified in advance and clearly documented. Typically, these out-of-tolerance conditions can be identified by means of:

Visual inspection by the operator (either at the completion of the entire order or as each part is completed).

A change in engineering specifications—due to an implemented ECO (engineering change order).

The occurrence of an "extraordinary" circumstance (e.g., the bin carrying the shop order has been dropped, or the shop order has undergone a wrong operation).

Inspection by machine sensors or visions.

A formal inspection.

---

[10] In addition to salvage and rework, there is also scrap. Because scrap passes out of the PAC system without further processing, it is not subject to the same dispatching considerations and is therefore ignored in this discussion.

The responsibility for identification should be clearly stated and known by all PAC personnel in advance.

Whenever an out-of-tolerance condition has been identified, the work should be stopped *immediately* and the problem corrected. The reason for the problem should be noted at the same time (while it is still fresh in the minds of the shop floor personnel) and recorded.

## Determination and Authorization

Once an order has been identified as failing to meet specifications, documented standard procedures should allow the appropriate employee (inspector, machine operator, plant foreman, etc.) to make a timely and appropriate decision as to how to proceed. One of the following options must be chosen:

Use as is (after making the appropriate repairs). Note that in some cases this decision cannot be made by the operator or inspector by himself. The decision may require calling on the engineering responsible for the item and its specifications.

Scrap.

Salvage (either completed or for its components).

Use for a different product. A part that fails to meet the standards for one product may still be appropriate for another product.

The management of rework, salvage, and scrap (which is not subject to the same dispatching considerations) often requires the cooperation of several different functional groups aside from the PAC system. These groups can include quality assurance, purchasing, production and inventory control, engineering, and manufacturing engineering. Representatives from these groups are frequently brought together in the form of a material review board (MRB), which is responsible for reviewing all problem orders and for deciding on an appropriate course of action for these orders.

Once the order has been identified and classified, it can be assigned to work centers by the dispatching process.

## Steps in Dispatching Rework and Salvage

The dispatching process for scrap and rework should be closely tied with accounting and quality assurance. The link with accounting is needed to report and track actual expense reporting versus actual reporting against standard operations. The link with quality assurance is needed to report and track quality problems and to identify the persistent quality problems occurring on the shop floor that require further management analysis and action.

The rework and scrap dispatching process consists of the following major steps:

1. *Capture the appropriate information.* To prevent future salvage and rework, the personnel responsible should capture and record the following information:

Part number
Work order number
Operation
Employee number
Machine or asset number
Resolution (i.e., whether the order was scrapped, reworked, or assigned to salvage)
Cause code
Defect code

This information must be recorded by means of a formal transaction (a report). Figure 18 provides a form for reporting quality problems, taken from the Control Division of the General Electric Locomotive Division. The figure also lists the cause and defect codes used by the Control Division in reporting the manufacturing losses.

2. *Make the appropriate modifications to the shop order.* Two decisions must be made when encountering scrap and rework. If a portion of a shop order does not meet standards, the PAC person must decide whether to keep the order together or to separate it into two separate orders. In general, the portion of the order requiring rework or salvage should be separated from the rest of the order and be given its own order identity (i.e., order number). This procedure need not be followed if the problem

# FIGURE 18 Inspector's Rejection Report and Manufacturing Loss Coding

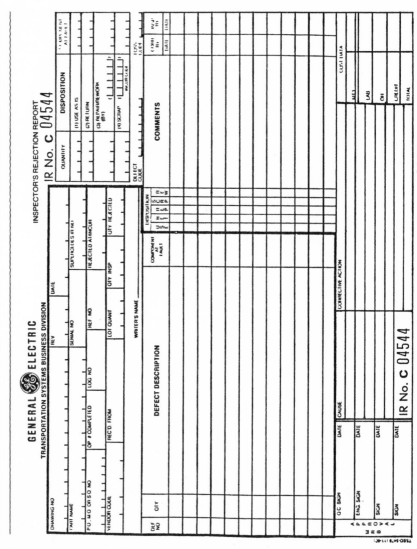

## FIGURE 18 *(continued)*

### CONTROL MANUFACTURING: MANUFACTURING LOSS CODING

Those persons assigning losses and applying them in inspection reports, production notices, repairable defect reports, or blue labor vouchers will use the following system of coding:

| | First Digit | | Second Digit | Group No. |
|---|---|---|---|---|
| 2XX | Rework/repair | X0X | Vendor | 1 |
| 3XX | Extra labor cost | X1X | Other than incur | |
| 4XX | Scrap | | manufacturing component | 8 |
| 8XX | Return to vendor | X2X | Engineering | 2 |
| 9XX | Use as is | X3X | Administration | 3 |
| | | X4X | Operator | 4 |
| | | X5X | Equipment | 5 |
| | | X6X | Test failure | 6 |
| | | X7X | Material handling | 7 |
| | | X8X | Digit unused | — |
| | | X9X | Product support | 9 |

Note: Purchasing concurrence is required before vendor responsibility assigned.

### THIRD DIGIT
(Select group corresponding to second digit selected.)

| Group 1 | Cause of Loss | Group 2 | (cont.) |
|---|---|---|---|
| XX1 | Not approved source | XX5 | Value improvement or suggestions |
| XX2 | Documentation incomplete | XX6 | Update to latest material or vendor part |
| XX3 | Unauthorized configuration change | XX7 | Product improvement |
| XX4 | Test data—missing, incomplete, or incorrect | XX8 | Factory request |
| | | XX9 | A.N. |
| XX5 | Not to latest drawing | XX0 | Drawing unclear |
| XX6 | Out of tolerance—rework internally | Group 3 | Cause of Loss |
| XX7 | Not to drawing—rework internally | XX1 | Bad tool design |
| | | XX2 | Tool crib error |
| XX8 | Scrap | XX3 | Planning incorrect |
| XX9 | Transportation/handling | XX4 | Administrative decision |
| XX0 | All other | XX5 | QC error |
| | | XX6 | Methods error |
| Group 2 | Cause of Loss | XX0 | All other |
| XX1 | Design error | | |
| XX2 | Drafting error | Group 4 | Cause of Loss |
| XX3 | Customer request | XX1 | Setup instruction needed |
| XX4 | Eliminate field problem or complaint | XX2 | Planning error |
| | | XX3 | Tooling error |

---

**FIGURE 18** *(concluded)*

---

| Group 4 | *(cont.)* | Group 7 | *Cause of Loss* |
|---|---|---|---|
| XX4 | Drawing unclear/error | XX1 | Improperly packaged/ |
| XX5 | Correct procedure not | | protected |
| | followed | XX2 | Improperly blocked/ |
| XX6 | Damaged | | braced |
| XX7 | Assembly error (training | XX3 | Lost or missing parts |
| | required) | XX4 | Damaged in move |
| XX8 | Machine problem | | (bumping, etc.) |
| XX9 | Process error | XX5 | Handling (drop, smash, |
| XX0 | Methods problem | | crush) |
| | | XX0 | All other |

| Group 5 | *Cause of Loss* | Group 8 | *Cause of Loss* |
|---|---|---|---|
| XX1 | Tool wear | XX1 | Fabrication shop |
| XX2 | Process or machine | XX2 | Machining shop |
| | incapable | XX3 | Assembly shop |
| XX3 | Machine breakdown | XX4 | Model shop |
| XX4 | Process limit exceeded | XX5 | Electronics shop |
| | (not operator controlled) | XX6 | Propulsion |
| XX5 | Defective fixture | XX7 | Building 7 |
| XX6 | Improper machine | XX8 | Buildings 10 and 12 |
| | maintenance | XX9 | Building 100 |
| | | XX0 | All other |

| Group 6 | *Cause of Loss* | Group 9 | *Cause of Loss* |
|---|---|---|---|
| XX1 | Out-of-tolerance output | XX1 | Extra setup |
| XX2 | Short circuit | XX2 | Material substitution |
| XX3 | Open circuit | XX3 | Lack of parts |
| XX4 | Mechanical failure | XX4 | Short cycle |
| XX5 | Test-induced failure | XX5 | Station capacity |
| XX6 | Test equipment | XX6 | Incorrect material |
| XX7 | Test procedure | XX7 | Incorrect drawing |
| XX8 | Drawing incorrect | XX8 | Drawing not supplied |
| XX9 | Vendor part | XX9 | Job book not supplied |
| XX0 | All other | XX0 | All other |

---

items can be corrected very quickly (without jeopardizing the on-time completion of the whole order).

The second decision involves the modification of the routing for rework/salvage operations. Except in cases of a minor correction (where the part may be recycled through the same operations), these operations have to be added to the existing work order or split out with the remaining standard operations as a salvage or rework work order. In many cases, the rework or salvage routing should already be present in the manufacturing routing file. Once added, these "new" operations can be handled by the PAC system as if they were normal operations.

3. *Add the due dates.* The modified order requires due dates (both for operations and the order) so that it can be managed by the PAC system. The order and operation due dates on the original shop order are often inapplicable to the rework or salvage order. The original operation due dates may not reflect the revised routings of rework. In the case of salvage, and the need that the original order due date was intended to satisfy can no longer be satisfied by salvage. Thus, the PAC system needs to assign order and operation due dates for both rework and salvage. These dates are used for determining priorities and for informing the planning system when inventory recovered from salvage operations will be available and when rework orders will be completed.

4. *Provide an estimate of hours.* The capacity effects generated by salvage and rework orders must *always* be identified and incorporated into capacity planning. If not, salvage and rework orders will tend to become disruptive as they compete for facilities with other orders. A facility with enough capacity for current "good" orders may not have enough capacity when salvage and rework orders are also considered.

5. *Capture the feedback.* Finally, a feedback mechanism must be present in the form of:

A quality history file that captures what went wrong and why it went wrong.

A corrective action program.

An program providing early warning of past defective conditions for both work orders and purchase orders.

## Other Considerations

In addition to the steps described above, the following factors should be considered when dispatching rework and salvage:

- The process for managing scrap, salvage, and rework must be integrated with the standard work order (i.e., shop order) system.
- Capacity should be set aside in advance for possible

salvage and rework as well as for "good" shop orders. Management should set aside a percentage of capacity for salvage and rework when planning.

- Scrap, salvage, and rework history should be summarized and reviewed on a regular basis (once a month, once a quarter). Such review is needed to identify persistent shop floor problems. For example, these problems may involve a particular worker, a specific machine (or tooling), or current problem standards. Problem orders should be identified and reviewed using an ABC form of analysis. That is, the orders causing most of the problems (e.g., between 50 and 80 percent) or the orders with dollar costs in excess of a certain breakpoint should be the candidates for further examination. Once identified, these orders should be assigned to a formal group for analysis and solution. Like the MRB, this group should consist of representatives from various involved functional groups (e.g., manufacturing engineering, engineering, quality assurance, PAC, and shop floor personnel).

- Orders involving scrap, salvage, and rework should be routinely evaluated and reviewed for efficiency and timeliness.

### Dispatching of Rework and Salvage Orders— Summary Comments

For most firms, scrap, salvage, and rework are realities of production. Not all orders are completed as required. Some orders are canceled because of scrap. Other orders require additional processing before they can satisfy product standards. These types of orders (primarily those involving salvage and rework) require a dispatching process that recognizes that they are different from "good" orders and therefore must be handled somewhat differently. Salvage and rework orders compete for capacity with other shop orders and need to be sequenced just like those other orders. The management of scrap, salvage, and rework must be an integral part of the PAC system. In many PAC systems, scrap, salvage, and rework are currently managed informally. Such management is not consistent with an effective PAC system.

# PAC Activities in the Job Shop: Data Collection/Monitoring

As previously noted, the information generated on the shop floor plays a critical role in the operation of the PAC system and in the entire manufacturing system. As a result, the PAC system is held responsible for the accurate and timely collection of that information from the shop floor and for its analysis. These responsibilities form the basis of the data collection/monitoring activities of the PAC system.

This general set of activities can be broken down into two segments: data collection and monitoring. Each of these segments has its own concerns and procedures.

## DATA COLLECTION

Data collection is an objective procedure that PAC personnel use to gather all of the information pertaining to the PAC system and its operation. Management requires accurate information to make well-informed, intelligent decisions in situations in which the actual results do not meet the plan. The data collection procedure therefore consists of two key activities:

- *Information Gathering:* the procedures used to gather information generated on the shop floor.
- *Information Verification and Editing:* the procedures used to verify the accuracy and completeness of the informa-

tion gathered and to correct any inaccuracies before that information becomes incorporated into the manufacturing data base.

Data collection is always a three-step process: information is first collected; then it is verified and corrected; and, finally, it is incorporated into the overall manufacturing data base.

## Information Gathering

In most systems, a great deal of activity takes place on the shop floor. If all of this activity were recorded, the amount of information generated might overwhelm the user. The availability of an excessive amount of detail might also reduce rather than increase the effectiveness of the resulting decisions made by management. Consequently, the problem facing PAC personnel is twofold:

1. What information should be collected (and how frequently)?
2. In what format should that information be recorded?

The solution to this problem cannot come from PAC personnel alone. The shop floor information generated by the PAC system is used extensively by other groups within the firm. Among the most important users are:

Design engineering
Cost accounting/finance
Manufacturing engineering
Marketing
Purchasing
Top management (as a test of how the business plan is being carried out)

Thus, the question of what information is to be collected should be made jointly by representatives of the PAC system and these other functional groups. In addition, the information collected should be provided in a format that satisfies the usage requirements of as many of the above groups as possible. The amount of modification that any of the above groups must carry out before it can use the information effectively should be kept to an absolute minimum. Any additional work of this kind that has to be done will tend to discourage rather than encourage its use.

Typically, the information collected on the shop floor by the PAC system reflects the following manufacturing concerns:

- Order location status. (Where is the order? How is it doing with respect to its order due date? What is happening to it currently?)
- Shop floor resource status. (What is the current condition of various work centers, tooling, material, and workers?)
- Quality and quality problems (and the reasons for these problems).
- Costs (actual and standard).
- Efficiency. (How well have the shop floor resources been used in making the order?)

**Information Frequently Collected.**   The collection of information from the shop floor should include:

Status of a given shop order.
On-order amounts completed on a given operation/order.
Current daily/weekly capacities by function or work center.
Labor-hours used for setup by clock number.
Labor-hours used for the actual operation by clock number.
Machine-hours used for setup by asset number (if applicable).
Machine-hours used for actual operations by asset number.
Indirect labor-hours by clock number.
Information needed for input/output control (i.e., number of jobs currently in queue by work center, number of jobs processed through each work center during the week, and number of unreleased orders by work center).
Requisitions and issues to a given operation/order.
Receipts of product into stores/finished stock.
Amount of scrap reported.
Rework/salvage operations required.
Alternative work centers/routings.
Split lots/send aheads.
Use of maintenance work orders by capital asset.

Scheduled maintenance of equipment.

Unscheduled downtime/absenteeism.

Tooling status (tooling kit lists with availability posting of unplanned operations notes explaining variances).

**Organization and Staffing.** Formal responsibility for information collection can be assigned to either timekeepers or machine operators. As a general rule, information collection is best undertaken by machine operators (i.e., direct employees) when they are armed with the proper real-time posting tools. Operators are most familiar with the status of both the shop order and the shop floor resources. They are best able to provide the PAC system with timely collection of data (e.g., at the completion of the order). They are also best able to record not only quantitative information (number of pieces produced, labor time required) but also qualitative information. That is, the operator is best able to record comments pertaining to the progress of the shop order and problems currently being experienced with it. Such information helps explain the quantitative information that has been captured. For example, longer processing times (quantitative information collected on the shop floor) can be best explained by allowing the operator to comment on the reasons. They may be the result of differences in the quality of the components supplied by a vendor.

**Method of Collecting Information.** A number of methods may be used to collect information from the shop floor. Each of these methods has different implications for the frequency of updating, timeliness, the possibility of operator input error, the maintenance of information accuracy, and the amount of operator time required. Five major methods are available.

1. *Verbal Communication.* This method of recording shop floor information is based on conversation that takes place between the operator and other PAC personnel. Verbal communication permits a great deal of qualitative and quantitative information to be passed on to the people involved in a very short time. Through verbal communication, for example, a department supervisor can find out that an order will not be completed on time

because of rejection of material or damage to a tool or machine almost as soon as such problems occur.

Verbal communication is best used as a supplement to other methods of information collection. If the situation surrounding a particular problem is not evident from a report, it can be quickly identified by talking with the people involved. Verbal communication should never be used by itself. As the only method of information collection, it is subject to a number of problems. For example, information collected in this way never gets entered into the manufacturing data base; over time, people forget details; and the PAC system becomes dependent on the knowledge and memories of people on the shop floor.

2. *Manual (Written Reports).* Information can be collected by means of manually filled reports that are then submitted for entry into the manufacturing data base. With this method, the operator is given a series of preprinted reports that he is required to fill in. These reports are turned in on a regular basis (e.g., at the end of a job, the end of a shift or the end of a week). Although the manual method of data collection is more reliable and dependable than verbal communication, it suffers from certain important limitations:

- It is time consuming (unless much of the descriptive information has already been preprinted).
- It is more prone to operator input error.
- Information is not added directly to the manufacturing data base. Instead, the reports generated by the operator must be entered by another group of PAC personnel. In many systems, for example, the operators turn in their reports to keypunch operators, who then enter the information. Such arrangements introduce the possibility of input errors from two sources (the operators and the keypunch operators). They also introduce a time lag between the time that information is turned in and the time that it is incorporated into the manufacturing data base.
- Data verification (checking the accuracy of the information entered) becomes an activity separate from data entry. Often the data is verified after it has been entered (often by someone else in the PAC system) into the manu-

facturing data base. The operator becomes aware of problems with the data after the fact and may no longer be able to resolve the problems (e.g., the operator has forgotten the circumstances surrounding the order).

As a general rule, manual data collection is most appropriate for small shops or for operations in which the manufacturing process is not complex. Manual data collection is more consistent with a batch system than with an on-line system.

3. *Preprinted Cards.* Another method of data collection is to provide the operator with a set of preprinted cards on which information from the work center is to be recorded and submitted. In the case of a shop order, this method of data collection involves the creation of a shop packet containing a ticket for each of the operations. At the start of an operation, the operator notes such information as the number of pieces received, his employee number, and the time at which the processing of the order was begun. At the completion of the operation, the operator notes the time when the order was completed, the number of pieces completed and passed on to the next operation, the number of pieces scrapped, and the number of pieces set aside for quality control (e.g., a decision must be made as to whether to rework, salvage, or scrap the parts). The operator may also record actual setup and run times on the card. The card is then turned in to either a keypunch operator or a dispatcher.

This method shares many of the same problems as the manual method. One major advantage that it offers, however, is fewer operator input errors. Since much of the order information is already printed on the card, there is no chance that the operator will copy it incorrectly.

4. *Data Collection Terminals.* This method links (by means of computer system) the data collection process directly to the manufacturing data base in an on-line setting. Data collection terminals can take one of two forms: card readers and CRTs (cathode-ray tubes). A card reader is simply a terminal through which a computer-generated card is first passed. The terminal then completes data collection by prompting the operator for certain items of information (e.g., operator number, number of

items completed, number of items scrapped). The CRT (or computer terminal) gathers information by presenting the operator with a screen that the operator fills in by entering responses at the keyboard. Compared with other procedures, this method of data collection offers the PAC system several significant advantages:

- It is less time consuming.
- It is less prone to input errors by the operator. Often, as soon as the operator enters the job number and location, the computer system retrieves all of the relevant order information (such as number of pieces begun and time released to the work center). The operator does not have to reenter this information.
- Data verification occurs at the same time as data collection. In the preceding methods, verifying the accuracy of the data was an activity separate from entering the data. Using data collection terminals, the computer system can force the operator to verify the data being entered. It can test for correct employee numbers and accounts. It can also test for certain conditions (such as differences between the number of pieces starting at the current operation and the number of pieces reported completed at the preceding operation or an excess in the number of pieces completed over the number of pieces started) and flag inconsistencies. If there are inconsistencies, the operator has two basic options: correct the data, or override the system and become responsible for explaining the factors that gave rise to the problem. Consider an error situation flagged by the computer in which the number of pieces scrapped plus the number of pieces completed does not equal the number of pieces started at an operation. The operator must either correct the incorrectly entered data or override the system by taking responsibility for the missing pieces. The computer system will not close out the transaction until all of the data has been entered correctly and all inconsistencies have been accounted for.
- The lead time from the time that information is entered into the terminal and the time that it becomes available to

the manufacturing data base is reduced substantially, and the entering of the information is more direct. The information no longer has to go through a keypunch operator.

In short, the use of data collection terminals is consistent with the presence of an on-line manufacturing data base that is updated in an ongoing fashion to reflect changes on the shop floor.

5. *Automated Identification.* A relatively new development in data collection, automated identification is a broad term encompassing procedures that encode information so that it can be read or transmitted by means of an electronic instrument (typically a scanning instrument) [11, p. 77]. This information is transmitted to a decoder that processes and records it. The most common automated identification systems are:

a. *Bar Coding.* Bar coding is currently the most commonly used automated identification system. A bar code consists of a series of alternating dark and light vertical bars. While all bar codes have a two-dimensional structure (height and width), width is the only dimension of concern since it is the width of each bar that represents digitally encoded information.[1] This information is encoded according to the specific coding scheme being used. The information contained in the bar code is transferred to the computer by passing a light scanner over the code. The scanner can be hand held, permanent with a fixed beam, or permanent with a moving beam.

b. *Optical Character Recognition (OCR).* Optical character recognition uses a set of codes that can be read by people and light pens. The information is read by a reading wand that must be in direct contact with the codes.

c. *Magnetic Strips.* Magnetic strips are a relatively new automated identification procedure in which information can be encoded at much higher density than that present in bar coding. The information contained in the strips can be read using either hand-held wands or slot readers.

---

[1]For more information on this topic, see A. Paradiso, "Bar Coding: A Brief Introduction," *Production and Inventory Management Review* 2, No. 6 (June 1982), pp. 16–19.

*d. Voice Recognition.* Voice recognition permits the employee to directly input data into the computer system *by voice.*[2]

Data collection using automated identification offers four major advantages:

- *Improved speed in transmitting information:* Few systems can match the speed with which a scanner is able to read, transmit, decode, and record information.
- *Reductions in the level of recording errors.*
- *Reductions in costs:* Automated identification can reduce the costs resulting from recording errors and slow information transmission speeds.
- *Simplified data collection procedures:* Using automated identification techniques greatly simplifies the process of physically collecting information on the shop floor. For example, the arrival of an order at a work center can be recorded by scanning the order's code. The computer system now knows the exact location of the order. When the order is ready to be processed, the code is scanned again. The second scan determines how long the order spent waiting in queue. By scanning the operator's number (represented by either a bar code or a magnetic strip), the work of the operator can also be recorded. When the operation has been completed, the order's code is scanned again. This information along with the number of pieces completed determines how long the order spent in process, the scrap rate, and the completion time.

Each of the methods for collecting information offers management distinct trade-offs among such factors as cost of operation, speed, accuracy, and ease of use. The specific method selected depends on such factors as the number of orders being processed, the manufacturing lead times, the size of the manufacturing process, and the need of the manufacturing system for timely and accurate data.

---

[2]For more information on this technology, see "Voice Recognition—Back Again and Better," *Modern Material Handling,* April 6, 1983, pp. 52–55.

**Other Considerations.** When collecting information, three factors should be kept in mind:

1. Information should be collected on a transaction-by-transaction basis. Transaction-by-transaction recording offers several important advantages. Information about the job is still fresh in the mind of the operator, with the result that data accuracy tends to be higher. Information about the location and status of orders is current. Finally, transaction-by-transaction recording imposes a discipline on shop floor personnel.

Transaction-by-transaction recording is most applicable to the job shop but may not be applicable in all production settings. In cases where the production volume is too high to report all operations, reporting by checkpoint operations is more appropriate. This procedure uses locations that are easily controlled from a reporting standpoint. In situations involving an assembly operation in which the flow from start to finish is very fast and the assembly lead time is very short, reporting against the order as a whole is another option to be considered. This option reports the start and completion of the order.

2. Information relating to the status and location of both shop orders and shop floor resources should be collected on an ongoing basis.

3. The data collection procedure should allow for the recording of both quantitative and qualitative information.

## Information Verification and Editing

The PAC system requires that *accurate* information be entered on a timely basis. Furthermore, the PAC system is held responsible for the accuracy of all information collected on the shop floor. Information collection provides the data but does not guarantee the accuracy of the data recorded. Verification and editing of the information gathered from the shop floor must be done before that information is incorporated into the manufacturing data base.

The need for verification is dependent on the type of data collection method being used. Such methods as automated identification and data collection terminals require less verification because in these methods the processes of data collection and data verification and editing occur almost simultaneously.

**When.** In general, the verification and editing of information should occur as soon as possible after the information has been recorded.

**Responsibility.** At a minimum, the responsibility for verifying and editing information should be assigned to the person recording it (the operator or the timekeeper) and to the department supervisor. The operator, for example, is responsible for entering information correctly. The department supervisor is responsible for the performance of his department. The accuracy of information is one indication of the performance of his department.

**Procedures for Information Verification and Editing.** Several procedures can be implemented to help in the verification and editing of information. The simplest and the easiest to implement is *visual verification*. That is, the supervisor reviews all reports submitted by personnel from his department. Each report is examined for completeness and to identify any errors in the information recorded. Overall, this is not an effective method for verifying information. It is time consuming for the supervisor, and it requires that the supervisor be very familiar with the work flowing into his department. Moreover, it will not catch most of the errors made. In general, visual verification is most applicable in small shops and in processes where the production process is simple and tends to be limited to one department.

A second procedure is "double entry." The operator or the keypunch operator enters the information twice. Any differences in the information entered are identified and corrected. Generally, this procedure will catch human input errors (e.g., entering 15 instead of 51). It will not, however, flag problems involving the reconciliation of data (e.g., the operator was sent 98 pieces but reported 105 pieces completed).

A third procedure is "software filtering," which is being used increasingly in firms with on-line data collection systems. Here, the computer system has programmed into it a series of tests that are applied against any information that is entered. These tests are intended to flag situations involving:

- *Reconciliation.* The information recorded cannot be reconciled with the information currently in the manufacturing data base. For example, the number of units reported as being completed plus the number of units scrapped plus the number of units being held by quality assurance is not equal to the number of units recorded as received at the work center.

- *Incomplete Recording of Information.* Not all of the required fields on the report have been filled in by the operator.
- *Incorrect Authorization.* Based on the information recorded, access was attempted by someone without proper authorization. For example, information was entered by someone whose employee number was not on the list of those employees with access.
- *Conflict with Standards.* Information was recorded that conflicts with the standards contained in the manufacturing data base. For example, the work center number entered is not the same as the one identified in the routings (standard or alternative).

The information recorded should be verified either at the terminal or as soon after the recording of the information as possible.

Irrespective of the verification procedure, any reports found to contain suspect information must be set aside and the problems corrected as soon as possible. Once the errors in reports have been identified and corrected, the information contained in these reports can be incorporated into the manufacturing data base.

## MONITORING

Monitoring is an ongoing activity intended to answer this question: How did the real world perform to the plan? Monitoring answers the question by continually drawing on information coming from the shop floor and by analyzing that information to identify situations where the differences between actual and planned performance are large enough to require management intervention. These "exceptions" are the major focus of monitoring.

Monitoring is best managed as a joint activity that involves, at a minimum, department supervisors and machine operators. These two groups play an important role in the identifying and solution of "exception" situations.

The information used in monitoring comes from several sources. Machine operators are a major source. In many instances, they can spot potential exceptions at their work centers. These potential exceptions are orders that are experiencing such problems as excessive scrap or rework levels or excessive setup or processing times. They can be identified on the basis of the job standards or the operator's experience. In most instances, however, potential exceptions are identified by examining the information recorded during data collection and comparing that actual performance with the standards. This analysis is often the responsibility of the department supervisor.

Information to be monitored on an exception basis should include:

Actual setup time to standard setup time.

Actual productive labor to standard labor-hours.

Pieces reported by later operations compared to count of pieces on the first operation.

Actual bill of material requisitioned and issued compared to the standard bill of material.

Actual operations completed by each work center on time compared to the total operations for each work center.

Actual orders completed on time compared to total orders completed.

Actual scrap reported on an operation basis compared to planned scrap.

Actual input released by work center compared to planned input.

Actual output released by work center compared to planned output.

Underloads and overloads by work center.

Unscheduled downtime of key equipment.

Actual downtime of equipment compared to scheduled downtime.

Abnormal operator absenteeism by department.

Value of additional operations required to satisfy rework/salvage conditions.

Actual receipts of finished stock by stores compared to order quantities.

Actual efficiencies of person and machine compared to planned efficiencies.

Actual utilization of person and machine compared to planned utilization.

Actual quality levels generated by person and machine.

Actual quantities by operation/stores (obtained from cycle counts) compared to the recorded quantities at these locations.

In general, the best justification for monitoring accurately is that this supports the real-time replanning that is needed to work a way out of conflicts!

# CHAPTER SEVEN

# PAC Activities in the Job Shop: Control/Feedback

It is a basic fact of PAC that things never go as planned. As soon as an order is released to the shop floor, changes take place that require reaction from PAC personnel. Some of these changes require little reaction; others, however, create problems that require a great deal of management intervention. These problems, which can involve not only orders but also shop floor resources, are out of control from the perspective of the PAC system. They are dealt with by the control/feedback activities of the PAC system, whose primary task is to bring them under control.

## BASIC TYPES OF SHOP FLOOR PROBLEMS

The out-of-control situations addressed by control/feedback can reflect one of two types of basic shop floor problems: shop order problems and shop floor resource problems.

1. Shop Order Problems. Such problems pertain to specific shop orders. In a shop order problem, the order cannot be completed as planned because of difficulties due to:

> Changes in order quantity (resulting from either a change in the customer order or the presence of scrap/salvage/rework).
> Changes in the due date (such a change may reflect, for example, a change in the timing of the customer's need).

Changes in product routing or product structure (such changes are frequently a result of engineering changes).

Past production practices (i.e., the order cannot currently meet either its due date or its cost standards due to problems at previous work centers).

Shop order problems can be created as a result of changes coming from outside the PAC system (e.g., from the master production schedule) or from within the PAC system (i.e., problems on the shop floor).

2. Shop Floor Resource Problems. Such problems affect the level of shop floor resources (tooling, machine capacity, personnel, and material) available for use by shop orders. Among the more frequent causes of shop floor resource problems are:

Absenteeism.

Turnover and the training of new operators (the learning curve for some operations may be significant and have a great effect on the capacity available over time).

Machine downtime (due to such factors as preventive maintenance and machine breakdown).

Material shortages (either temporary due to delays in handling material or permanent as in the case of lost material).

Tooling shortages/breakdowns.

Acts of God (e.g., fire or flooding).

These two types of problems should not be viewed as mutually exclusive. A specific out-of-control situation may reflect one or both types.

## PURPOSES OF CONTROL/FEEDBACK

Control/feedback has four basic purposes:

1. Identifying the shop floor problems to be corrected.
2. Problem correction.
3. Long-term problem resolution.
4. Information feedback.

Often many problems are present in a shop at a given point in time. Some of the problems are critical and require immediate action; others are serious but not critical, so action on them can be delayed until the critical problems have been solved; and still others are no more than minor aggravations that require little or no management intervention. The first purpose of control/feedback is to identify the relative urgency of action on each of the shop floor problems. The critical problems must be brought to the top and solved first.

The second purpose of control/feedback is simply that of correcting problems and bringing them under control. This purpose does not necessarily address the underlying causes of problems. If a shop order is late, control/feedback may add more capacity in the form of overtime and subcontracting in order to get the order completed on time. This may not eliminate the cause of the problem, which in the case of the late order, may lie with a late engineering change.

Bringing problems under control, while important, is not enough. If a problem is a symptom pointing to a persistent, long-term cause, control/feedback must identify that cause and eliminate it. It is this identification and elimination of underlying causes so as to prevent a recurrence of problems that differentiates effective control/feedback from ineffective expediting.

Finally, control/feedback keeps other affected groups (such as master scheduling) aware of the situation on the shop floor and warns them of situations in which production goals such as order due dates will not be met.

## EVENTS TRIGGERING CONTROL/FEEDBACK

Control/feedback is typically initiated for the following reasons:

1. The shop order requirements have been changed. As a result of an engineering change or a customer-requested change, the order can no longer be completed on time and still meet the new requirements.

2. Data collection/monitoring has identified situations involving shop orders or shop floor resources in which the actual performance lags behind the planned performance.

3. Information received from the shop floor has identified a situation requiring immediate action (e.g., an operator has informed the department supervisor of damage to a critical tool).

4. The periodic review of summary reports produced by the PAC system points to problems on the shop floor.

5. As a result of direct inquiries about the progress of an order, management is trying to improve performance on that order, to overcome delays or remove bottlenecks affecting the order's progress. The extent to which these actions are carried out in response to a direct inquiry will depend on such factors as the importance of the customer making the request and the importance of the results to the customer.

As with every other PAC activity, control/feedback must be initiated by the formal system. It must be a response to information that comes from the formal system rather than the result of a "gut" feeling.

## PERSONNEL INVOLVEMENT IN CONTROL/FEEDBACK

As a general rule, control/feedback should be initiated at the lowest level of the PAC system. This means that in many instances the machine operator initiates control/feedback; in some instances, however, control/feedback is initiated by either the department supervisor or the dispatcher. Whoever within the PAC system recognizes the need for corrective action should initiate the control/feedback process.

A critical feature of control/feedback is that it places a premium on joint decision making. In some instances, the person who recognizes the need for corrective action may lack the authority to introduce the appropriate corrective action and must therefore work with people who have the necessary authority. For example, a department supervisor who is unable to bring an order back on schedule must work with the master scheduler in order to change the order due date. In other instances, joint decision making is required to bring together the various kinds of expertise needed to solve a problem. For example, the solution of a quality problem may require the cooperation of quality assurance (quality standards), manufacturing engineering (methods), engineering (product design), warehousing (material storage), and purchasing (purchased materials).

## STEPS IN THE CONTROL/FEEDBACK PROCESS

Control/feedback can be broken down into the following major steps:

1. *Establish the procedures for flagging out-of-control situations.* PAC personnel should focus only on situations that are considered critical. Management must have in place methods for separating noncritical situations from critical situations. A method particularly applicable in computer-based systems is to establish tolerances for the various reports. The tolerances should be agreed on by management and may be stated in such terms as these: "a critical shop order is one that is 20 days or more behind schedule," or "a critical work order is one that is generating an average product defective rate (scrap, rework, salvage) in excess of 10 percent." The computer system will then flag all transactions that fall outside the tolerances and will typically report these transactions in an "exception report." The tolerances can be set using statistical distributions (e.g., the normal distribution), or they can be negotiated. As an example of the latter approach, the maximum number of days late can be set to reflect a trade-off between marketing's perception of the costs of delivering an order late and manufacturing's evaluation of the costs of bringing the order in on time. On-time delivery may be considered crucial to the firm because of a corporate strategy that emphasizes it (as in the case of Steelcase, Inc. of Grand Rapids, Michigan). As a result, on-time delivery may far outweigh any costs incurred by production.

2. *Prioritize the critical situations.* Next, the critical situations identified in the first step must be rank-ordered, with the most critical situation at the top. One method by which such a ranking can be achieved is an ABC analysis approach. That is, the people involved try to identify the 20 percent of situations that are responsible for over 50 percent of their difficulties. The positioning of a critical situation can reflect both qualitative and quantitative considerations. In the case of late shop orders, for example, the urgency of an order can be based on the number of days that the order is behind schedule. This factor can then be modified to take into account the importance of the customer.

Another method is simply to identify one or two attributes of interest and to rank all of the jobs in terms of those attributes. This approach is best illustrated by the procedures used at the Control Manufacturing Division, General Electric Erie Facility. Figure 19 provides an example of a dispatch list. The dispatch list does not simply provide a basis for sequencing orders. More important, it identifies critically late jobs. The orders that are the

# FIGURE 19 Daily Dispatch List

```
TRANS NO 6GRO10            SHOP FLOOR CONTROL               06/18/85  12:09
                           DAILY DISPATCH LIST
                        WORK STA 0719  ACTIVE JOBS
```

| | OPER | REPORT | | | | CURRENT | PREVIOUS DAYS | |
| SLAC BOOK | QTY | QTY | DRAWING | DESC | LOC | STA OPR | STA OPR | I/A |
|---|---|---|---|---|---|---|---|---|
| 55- 721826 | 1129 | 1124* | 6700392G1 | CONTACT | 719 | 0719 005 | 0831 001 | 8 |
| 17- 721829 | 1500 | 1500 | 8860749G1 | FINGER | | 0719 020 | 0831 001 | 5 |
| 17- 721824 | 2300 | 2300 | 8807882G1 | CONTACT | M/S | 0719 005 | 0831 001 | 21 |
| 13- 723746 | 1500 | 1500 | 8860749G1 | FINGER | | 0719 020 | 0831 001 | 5 |
| 12- 722518 | 2300 | 2300 | 8807882G1 | CONTACT | M/S | 0719 005 | 0831 001 | 21 |
| 12- 723694 | 1610 | 1610 | 6700549G1 | CONT ASM | | 0719 010 | 0721 005 | 3 |
| 12- 722519 | 2300 | 2300 | 8807882G1 | CONTACT | M/S | 0719 005 | 0831 001 | 21 |
| 7- 725056 | 2300 | 2300 | 8807882G1 | CONTACT | | 0719 005 | 0831 001 | 8 |
| 7- 725057 | 2300 | 2300 | 8807882G1 | CONTACT | | 0719 005 | 0831 001 | 8 |
| 6- 723556 | 2500 | 2500 | 9964601G2 | BOX ASM | | 0719 025 | 0160 020 | 1 |
| 5- 725063 | 1000 | 1000 | 8867935G1 | FRAME ASM | | 0719 005 | 0831 001 | 12 |
| 5- 724915 | 28 | 28 | 41D757119G2 | BASE | | 0719 030 | 0168 015 | 7 |

```
*---------------------------HOLD UP JOBS-------------------------------*

CODE 04  25  42  30  **
NO   21   1   1   1   1

                    TOTAL JOBS    21
```

## FIGURE 19 (concluded)

** In addition to the 21 jobs active, there are 24 jobs inactive on holdup codes.

1. Input 010, work station & press new line or enter key.
   Example: 010,0719
   Output is about 10-13 lines of data and then a summary.

2. Input 010, work station & number of lines wanted; press new line or enter key.
   Example: 010,0719017
   Output is 17 lines of data & then a summary as in 1 above.

3. Input 010, work station & ALL; press new line or enter key.
   Example: 010,0719ALL
   Output is all items active for the work station & total plus summary of inactive jobs.

4. If it is a dispatch coded operation (central dispatching in 42-7 only) the 01 status means that the job is in the carousel waiting to be dispatched to the work station.

5. The * means the job is on multiple holdup codes at that operation/work station.

furthest behind schedule are always found at the top. These are the orders which management tries to control by ensuring that they are always moving (i.e., the days inactive indicator is low). Each week, the top-priority orders for each work center are ranked in terms of slack (Figure 20). These reports provide the large negative slack jobs with a great deal of visibility. They indicate which orders are important and why.

3. *Identify what has to be done to bring the critical problems under control.* Next, methods of solving the problem in the short term must be evaluated. This evaluation consists of (1) identifying what alternatives are available and (2) determining whether these alternatives are sufficient. This evaluation can be done by the person who first identified the problem (e.g., the operator or the supervisor), or it can be done in a committee consisting of representatives from the various affected groups (e.g., master scheduling, purchasing, quality assurance, and manufacturing engineering).

The solution process for Step 3 is hierarchical. This step tends to present the solution process as a series of hierarchical steps. That is, the supervisor can typically attack problems with such tools as overtime, part time, subcontracting, or rearrangement of the work force. The supervisor cannot, however, change the order due date. This authority is vested in the master scheduler. If the options available to the supervisor are not adequate to solve a problem, he must go to the next level and contact the master scheduler. Each level will try to exhaust the options available to it before going to the next higher level.

4. *Implement the short-term solution.* Having identified a solution that can correct the problem in the short term, the next step is to implement that solution.

5. *Review the problem to identify its underlying causes.* Each problem solved must be reviewed to identify the reasons for its occurrence. In those cases where a problem is the result of short-term factors (e.g., a new operator who is still learning how to operate the equipment), control/feedback can stop here. The problem is not likely to recur. However, in cases where a problem points to persistent underlying causes, control/feedback must identify those causes. They must then be eliminated to prevent a recurrence of the problem. The process of identifying the under-

# FIGURE 20 Top-Priority Orders

WORK CENTER 126-0930          DESCRIPTION CINCINNATI MTX

| DAYS E/L | SWAN | PART NUMBER | | DESCRIPTION | LOC | DUE DTE | SCHEDULED-THIS-W/C OPER | ST | -S/U | --RUN- | --COMING-FROM--- OPER | -W/C- ST AWAY | HRS | -LAST-MOVE-REPORTED- OPER | -W/C- | --QTY- | ORDER WAI --QTY- | DAY |
|---|---|---|---|---|---|---|---|---|---|---|---|---|---|---|---|---|---|---|
| 13- | 145201A | A28784 | 003 | FRAME | ONC | 999 | 0070 | 40 | 7.5 | 3.1 | COMPLETED | | | 0070 | 126-0343 | 24 | 24 | |
| 7 | 141358A | A28784 | 003 | FRAME | ONC | 020 | 0140 | 30 | 1.8 | 24.6 | SSET- 6.3 SRUN- | | 25.4 | 0070 | 126-0343 | 24 | 24 | |
| 38 | 149823A | A28784 | 003 | FRAME | ONC | 060 | 0110 | 30 | -2.2 | 3.3 | SSET- 7.3 SRUN- | | 25.6 | 0070 | 126-0343 | 24 | 24 | |
| 13- | 145201A | A28784 | 003 | FRAME | ONC | 999 | 0140 | 20 | 6.3 | 25.4 | AVAILABLE | | | 0070 | 126-0343 | 24 | 24 | |
| 16 | 149815A | A28784 | 003 | FRAME | ONC | 040 | 0110 | 20 | 7.3 | 25.6 | AVAILABLE | | | 0070 | 126-0343 | 24 | 24 | |
| 30 | 144089A | A28784 | 003 | FRAME | ONC | 040 | 0140 | 20 | 6.3 | 23.3 | AVAILABLE | | | 0070 | 126-0343 | 22 | 22 | |
| 52 | 126797A | A22391 | 001 | PROFILE | ONC | 010 | 0120 | 20 | 3.0 | 14.0 | AVAILABLE | | | 0120 | 126-0343 | 24 | 24 | |
| 52 | 138727A | A22391 | 001 | PROFILE | ONC | 010 | 0120 | 20 | 3.0 | 14.0 | AVAILABLE | | | 0120 | 126-0343 | 24 | 24 | 1 |
| 18 | 157677A | A28784 | 003 | FRAME | P15 | 060 | 0070 | 10 | 7.5 | 34.2 | 0060 123-0250 | 20 | | 0040 | 123-0210 | 12 | 24 | |

WORK CENTER 126-0930   CAPACITY= 58   CRIT Q HRS= 45   TTL LOAD HRS= 194   CRIT Q DAYS= 0.8   TTL Q DAYS= 3.4

**FIGURE 20 (concluded)**

SHOP FLOOR CONTROL
TOP PRIORITY
FOR AREA 06

09/06/84 06:48

| SLAC ST | BOOK | ORDER QTY | REPORT QTY | DRAWING NUMBER | DESC LOC | CURRENT WORK STA | OPR NO | PREVIOUS WORK STA | OPR NO | DAYS I/A |
|---|---|---|---|---|---|---|---|---|---|---|
| 213- 30 | 632469 | 12 | 12 | 41R997693G1 | HARNESS DLC | 0302 | 005 | 0807 | 001 | 30 |
| 197- | EB8137 | 56 | 56 | 41B566565G1 | | 0347 | 002 | 0805 | 001 | 24 |
| 137- | 637415 | 4000 | 3000 | 41A257901P6 | NAME PLATE OK | 0343 | 005 | 0807 | 001 | 9 |
| 137- | 637407 | 4000 | 3000 | 41A257901P12 | NAME PLATE OK | 0343 | 005 | 0807 | 001 | 9 |
| 132- | 637414 | 4000 | 3500 | 41A257901P6 | NAME PLATE OK | 0343 | 005 | 0807 | 001 | 9 |
| 132- | 637406 | 4000 | 2800 | 41A257901P12 | NAME PLATE OK | 0343 | 005 | 0807 | 001 | 9 |
| 127- | 637405 | 4000 | 3000 | 41A257901P12 | NAME PLATE OK | 0343 | 005 | 0807 | 001 | 9 |
| 122- | 662501 | 20000 | 10000 | 41A274679G2 | PIN TO PIN OK | 0321 | 005 | 0807 | 001 | 4 |
| 121- | 104393 | 12 | 12 | 165V837P1 | IND PL | 0341 | 020 | 0160 | 019 | 1 |
| 116- 30 | 643467 | 50 | 50 | 41A255325P3 | NAMEPLATE | 0342 | 005 | 0807 | 001 | 94 |

| | | | DLC | | |
|---|---|---|---|---|---|
| 101- | 645034 | 50 | 41A278832P1 | NAMEPLATE | 0342 005 0807 001 81 |
| 98- | 669124 | 10 | 41A322010AUG102 | WIRES | 0345 010 0302 005 13 |
| | | | | OK | |
| 91- | 647586 | 10 | 41A278832P1 | NAMEPLATE | 0342 005 0807 001 72 |
| 86- | 669120 | 6 | 41A322010BCG100 | WIRE LIST | 0345 020 0302 015 13 |
| | | | | OK | |
| 77- | 669126 | 9 | 41A322010AUG101 | WIRES | 0345 010 0302 005 13 |

A. TO OBTAIN THIS PROMPT:

1. INPUT 016,0151,06 & NEW LINE OR ENTER KEY (AUX AFTER IF YOU WANT IT
   PRINTED)

   OUTPUT: TOP JOBS IN DECLINING ORDER

2. A MAXIMUM OF FIVE AREA CODES CAN BE INPUT AT ONE TIME

   EXAMPLE: 016,0151,02,03,04,05,06

lying causes of a problem is best done in a committee drawn from the various related groups within the firm.

6. *Periodically review progress on eliminating the identified underlying causes.* Once a solution has been identified and implemented, the effectiveness of the solution must be reviewed periodically. One purpose of such review is to ensure that the problems attributed to the identified causes are no longer occurring.

7. *Ensure that the other areas are kept aware of the problems experienced on the shop floor and of the actions being taken to correct these problems.* By keeping groups such as marketing aware of any difficulties on the shop floor, control/feedback tries to avoid the "surprises" that occur if an order expected by marketing is not available when marketing thought it would be.

## CORRECTIVE ACTIONS AVAILABLE

A number of corrective actions are available to PAC personnel when coping with out-of-control situations. The options used depend greatly on the type of shop floor problem being faced. In the case of shop order problems, for example, the options typically available include:

- *Operation Overlapping.* This option is used in the case of order lateness. The use of operation overlaps suspends the requirement that the shop order move from one operation to the next as a *completed lot.* The lead time is compressed by not having the order wait for the completion of the last item before it can proceed to the next operation.
- *Operation Splitting.* This approach tries to correct the status of a critical shop order by performing the order in parallel at one operation by assigning more machines or more workers to the order [6].
- *Lot Splitting.* Lot splitting attempts to ensure order availability by breaking the critical short order into several smaller lots. Some of these lots are pushed ahead, while the remainder are allowed to proceed normally [6, p. 34].
- *Alternative Operations and Routings.* In certain cases where the standard machines or routings are not available (due to machine breakdowns or heavy use), other machines or routings can be used.

- *Order Cancellation.* In some cases, the problem order can simply be canceled. Such cancellation may reflect a customer request, or, in the case of excessive scrap/salvage/rework, it may be more cost efficient to throw out an entire order and start over instead of trying to correct the problems in the existing batch.
- *Subcontracting/purchasing Components.*

Shop floor resource problems, on the other hand, can be attacked by using one or more of the following options:

Change in the work pace. Changing the work pace does not always involve speeding up the pace. In certain cases where a work center is producing parts faster than other centers can use them, the answer might be to slow down the work pace.

Overtime.

Part time.

Safety capacity. A portion of the total capacity is not used or is allocated to production on average. This excess capacity is then available to deal with unexpected changes in the level of demand or capacity (e.g., due to worker illness).

Alternative operations or routings.

Subcontracting.

Lot splitting.

Each of the above options brings with it a set of costs and a set of limitations. These costs and limitations must be weighed against the types of problems faced and the importance of solving them. In cases where the costs of the options exceed the benefits they provide, the alternative of not doing anything might be the appropriate one to choose.

## OTHER CONSIDERATIONS

There are several other considerations PAC personnel should keep in mind when structuring and operating control/feedback activities. Among the most significant of these considerations are the following:

1. The interval between the time a problem is identified and the time it is solved should be as small as possible. In general, the

longer that interval, the more difficult and expensive it is to solve the problem. Ultimately, shop floor problems should be solved at the work center when they occur.

2. Critical shop floor problems should always be highly visible to everyone involved. Everyone should constantly be reminded of the need to bring these problems under control. This can be done by incorporating an appropriate ranking procedure into the reporting system (which displays the most critical jobs or work centers at or near the top). It can also be done by periodically generating reports that look only at problems.

3. Shop floor personnel should know in advance what options they can use to resolve problems and the order in which these options are to be used. Management must work with shop floor personnel in identifying the available options, the conditions under which these options are to be applied, and the general sequence in which they are to be used. Establishing these options in advance enhances the operation of the PAC system in several ways. This simplifies the activities of the shop floor personnel since they know in advance what they can and cannot do, and when. It reduces uncertainty involving the operation of the PAC system since everyone in the firm now knows how shop floor personnel will respond to out-of-control situations. Finally, when the order due date has to be changed, it enables the planners to know exactly what actions the shop floor personnel took before they asked for the change.

4. The reporting system must be structured to provide shop floor personnel with appropriate types of access to information. Too much information may be worse than not enough information. An effectively structured information system is one in which information is initially provided in the form of summaries. These summaries provide a general indication of the presence or absence of problems on the shop floor. Once a problem has been identified, the shop floor personnel can look at more detailed reports. They can obtain more and more detail from the system until they feel that they understand the problem and its causes. In this approach, the detail is provided only when the user needs it and asks for it.

5. Expediting can be used effectively *only* if it is tightly controlled and if it is directed at reducing the need for expediting. In many PAC systems, however, expediting is largely ineffective be-

cause it occurs too frequently, so that the expediters and the priorities assigned by them tend to lose validity in the eyes of shop floor personnel, and because it is an incomplete activity. Expediters tend to focus on symptoms instead of finding a solution to the problems that gave rise to the need for expediting. Thus, expediters tend to perpetuate the need for future expediting.

6. Procedures for the handling of scrap/salvage/rework should be built into the control/feedback activities. Classifying an order (or a portion of an order) as scrap/salvage/rework is best handled within control/feedback. In practice, scrap/salvage/rework is best handled by a material review board (MRB) with representatives drawn from PAC, engineering, manufacturing engineering, quality assurance, master scheduling, and warehousing. The MRB should meet regularly (once a day if possible) and review all orders routed to it for classification. It should be responsible for the disposition of order as well as the assignment of the revised due date (if applicable). The procedures used should conform to the guidelines set down in this section.

## CONTROL/FEEDBACK: CONCLUDING REMARKS

Control/feedback plays an important role in the operation of PAC, for it is the method by which the PAC system replans its way out of conflicts. Effective control/feedback prevents the recurrence of shop floor problems.

# CHAPTER EIGHT

# PAC Activities in the Job Shop: Order Disposition

The last major set of PAC activities is order disposition. Order disposition describes all of the activities that PAC personnel must engage in to close out an order and to relieve the PAC system of responsibility for it. At this stage, the PAC system is faced by a situation in which no further processing is possible on a manufacturing order. Such a situation may occur for several reasons:

The order has been completed as planned.

The order has been completed as either order salvage or component salvage.

The order has been scrapped.

At this point, the PAC system must close out the order. No further shop floor resources can be assigned to the order. The work authorization issued during the order review/release phase of PAC must now be withdrawn.

## PURPOSES OF ORDER DISPOSITION

Order disposition fulfills several important purposes for the PAC system and the manufacturing planning system. These are:

1. Order relief.
2. Notification of order availability.

3. Overall evaluation of the PAC system's performance on the shop order.
4. Identification and resolution of any "unexplained" variances.
5. Identification of persistent shop floor problems.

The first purpose is straightforward. During the order disposition phase, the PAC system indicates to the manufacturing system that the shop order has been completed. Control over the order is now passed from the PAC system, typically to either inventory control (in the case of a completed shop order or salvage) or material control (in the case of scrap). At this point, the order increases either the on-hand inventory balance or the expense account (as in the case of scrap).

Closely linked to this first purpose is the second purpose, the notification of order availability. During order disposition, on completion of a shop order, the PAC system indicates the availability of the order by adjusting the inventory records of the appropriate accounts. The in-process quantity is reduced, while the on-hand component quantities are increased. These two changes need not be completely offsetting in those cases where untraceable open quantities are present.

In processing the manufacturing order, the PAC system draws on the shop resources under its control. Once the order has been completed, the PAC system must be evaluated in terms of how efficiently these resources were used. This evaluation forms the basis for the third purpose.

The fourth purpose of order disposition is variance analysis. In evaluating the performance of the PAC system, the actual results are compared with standards. The resulting variances are reviewed, particular attention being given to unfavorable variances. It is critical that these variances be explained. PAC personnel must know whether these variances indicate a "onetime" situation or whether they indicate a much deeper problem (e.g., inapplicable work standards). If an unfavorable variance is not adequately explained, the PAC system loses much of its ability to formulate and implement effective corrective actions. What cannot be explained cannot be corrected.

The fifth and final purpose of order disposition is to identify and correct persistent shop floor problems on the basis of the information obtained from the variance analysis. (For example, excessively large queues or a persistent inability to meet due dates may indicate a capacity problem.) This final purpose requires that PAC personnel not limit themselves to record-keeping but that they also examine and monitor over time the information accumulated at the completion of the shop order.

## EVENTS TRIGGERING ORDER DISPOSITION

Order disposition is typically initiated for the following reasons:

1. An engineering change, customer cancellation or forecast change causes a shop order to be terminated immediately.
2. A shop order is terminated and directed to order disposition as scrap.
3. The outstanding balance yet to be completed on a shop order is within an acceptable tolerance. That tolerance should be a policy previously set by management. Such a policy might state, for example, that any order whose outstanding balance is within plus or minus 10 percent should be closed out. By setting such a policy in advance, management can make shop orders available earlier than they would be if an entire order had to be completed in order to close out the order.
4. The total quantity of an order is ultimately received into the stockroom.
5. A review of the open orders is made by the planners to identify candidates for closure. In this review, the planners must consider the quantity received to stock and the quantity still open but not traceable.

Like the other PAC activities, order disposition must be initiated by a formal transaction. This transaction may originate from either the manufacturing planning system (as in the case of a forecast change or a customer cancellation) or the PAC system (as in the case of scrap or the receipt of a total order quantity into stock). It is therefore crucial that management establish in advance the conditions under which a shop order is to be closed and that management communicate these conditions to the shop floor personnel involved.

## AUTHORITY FOR ORDER DISPOSITION

As with the other PAC activities, someone within the PAC system should be held accountable for order disposition. This person should be expected to review all shop orders to be closed to:

Determine whether they satisfy the conditions for order disposition.

Complete their final evaluation by comparing the actual results with the standards.

Review all variances and provide adequate and appropriate explanations of those variances wherever possible.

In most cases, the responsibility for closing out is given to an individual, frequently someone from production control (e.g., a parts planner). In some cases, the supervisor of the department in which an order is completed is held responsible for closing it out; in other cases, the stockroom supervisor is required to close out an order on its receipt into stock. We will talk about production control and the parts planner when identifying that PAC person directly responsible for order disposition.

In completing the review of a shop order to be closed, the parts planner indicates the completion of the order by making the appropriate data base entries. A shop order is *never* closed out until the parts planner is satisfied that it has met all of the conditions indicated in this section's discussion.

## ORDER DISPOSITION REVIEW

After production control closes out an order, there should be an accounting review of order disposition. This review should consist of a pro forma order completion that covers:

1. Labor variances.
2. Material variances.
3. Scrap.
4. Rework.
5. Labor efficiency.
6. Labor utilization.
7. Machine efficiencies.
8. Machine utilizations.

9. Engineering variances caused by ECNs (engineering change notices).

If the variances identified by this review are "unreasonable" (i.e., they exceed some predetermined tolerance), the shop order should be reopened in order to accumulate additional data. In all cases, the shop order should drop off the system into history after the passage of a predetermined interval (e.g., a month or a year). This interval should be established by accounting in consultation with personnel from PAC and production control. The interval should reflect such considerations as the average manufacturing lead times, the number of orders processed per week, the importance of quality control, and the presence of governmental regulation. For example, the Consumer Healthcare Division of Miles Laboratories allows shop orders to age off the active manufacturing data base after five years. This interval is in part the result of strict governmental regulation.

At a minimum, the recorded history of a shop order must contain:

Quantity received and quantity begun.
Scheduled due date.
Actual completion date.
Actual costs, with comparison to the standard costs.
Quality information.

Finally, the order closed must be reviewed to determine the accuracy of:

1. Routing standards.
2. Bill of material accuracy.
3. Actual costs compared to standard costs.

The closing out of a shop order should be communicated to the rest of the manufacturing system by means of either hard copy or an on-line transaction. While a verbal indication of an order disposition is possible (especially in small shops), this method of communication should be avoided whenever possible to ensure that data bases are updated and appropriate action is taken.

## OTHER CONSIDERATIONS

In addition to the preceding factors, several other considerations should always be kept in mind during the order disposition phase of the PAC system. These are:

- *Unreleased shop floor resources should be released immediately.* On completion of a shop order and its disposition out of the PAC system, any shop floor resources currently assigned to the shop order and not consumed, such as material or tooling, should be released as soon as possible. These resources are no longer needed by the completed order and should be made available to shop orders yet to be completed.

- *A shop order should be closed out as quickly as possible and as soon as possible after the completion of the last operation on the shop floor.* Order disposition should not be a difficult or time-consuming activity for the PAC system. Information on the shop order and its progress has been accumulated on an ongoing basis. At the conclusion of every transaction, data has been collected and the activity monitored. As a result, order disposition becomes simply a final check and "look" at the shop order.

  Order disposition should be done as quickly as possible in order to make the order available to the manufacturing system as soon as possible. It should also be done immediately after the completion of the last operation, because any unresolved variances are most easily explained if the events surrounding an order are still fresh in the minds of shop floor personnel. As the time between the last operation and the order closing grows, people forget the details and the quality of the information on such matters deteriorates.

- *Order dispositions should be reviewed on a regular basis.* The parts planner should regularly review the history of all orders completed during, say, the last month or quarter. The purpose of this review is to identify any persistent and recurrent problems involving either orders (e.g., standards) or shop floor resources (e.g., capacity). Once such problems have been identified, the parts planner should pass on this information to the involved parties (e.g., engineering or accounting in the case of questionable standards). The information should form the basis for initiating corrective actions.

In addition to uncovering new problems, the parts planner should also review the progress on problems identified in the last review. This review of past problems is an important form of feedback. If a problem has been corrected, the review informs the involved groups that their corrective actions were effective. If a problem persists, the involved groups know that their corrective actions were insufficient and that alternative actions are needed. In either case, this regular review keeps everyone's focus on solving PAC problems.

# CHAPTER NINE

# Performance Evaluation and Measurement and Other Issues in PAC

Central to the last three PAC activities (data collection/monitoring, control/feedback, and order disposition) is the issue of setting and using performance measures. A performance measure is a means by which actions taking place on the shop floor are observed, measured, and subsequently evaluated.

## PURPOSES OF PERFORMANCE MEASURES

"Good" performance measures should provide shop floor personnel with means of:

1. *Communicating the major objectives of the PAC system.* The performance measures should emphasize the major objectives of the PAC system. Performance measures that do this continually educate the users on what the users have to do well for the PAC system to perform effectively. In a PAC system where on-time delivery is important, an appropriate performance measure for a work center is "percentage of operation due dates met."

2. *Recording actions.* The performance measures should provide the PAC system with means by which the performance of shop floor personnel is recorded. Such a permanent record is fundamental to any system based on accountability.

3. *Identifying potential shop floor problems.* The performance measures should help the user identify potential problems before these problems become serious. In other words, good performance measures should provide the user with an "early warning" system.

4. *Correcting problems.* Not only should the performance measures help the user identify potential problems; they should also be the starting point by which the user corrects problems uncovered by the measures. For example, the attempts of an operator to improve operations at a work center might begin with an unfavorable cost variance.

5. *Evaluation.* The performance measures should provide the PAC system with means of evaluating the actions of shop floor personnel on a regular basis. This is the purpose that is most frequently associated with performance measures.

A well-thought-out and integrated set of performance measures is an important component of any effective PAC system.

## CHARACTERISTICS OF GOOD PERFORMANCE MEASURES

Good performance measures incorporate the following considerations:

1. *Simple to use.*
2. *Simple to understand.*
3. *Consistent with the objectives of the PAC.* The performance measures should focus on evaluating how well specific PAC objectives are implemented on the shop floor (e.g., at the work center). The performance measures should always be linked to the PAC objectives.
4. *Generate meaningful measures.* The performance measures should generate results that are readily understood by the user. If the user can understand the measures, he can use the information they generate and act on it.
5. *Limited in number.* Ideally, the user should be given only a few (no more than four) performance measures. A few measures provide the user with a well-defined

focus, so that there is no ambiguity over what the user must do well. As more measures are added, it becomes more difficult for the user to satisfy the growing number of measures and the user tends to become more confused as he tries to identify which of the measures are most important.

6. *Provide rapid and timely feedback.* The results of the performance measures should be made available on a timely basis (e.g., at the end of every day or shift) so that the user can identify and correct problems before they worsen.

7. *Differentiate between "inherited" problems and problems directly attributable to the actions of the person being measured.* A problem identified at a given work center can often be broken into two components. One component is the result of problems encountered at upstream work centers. The other component reflects the problems encountered at the given work center. The performance measures should be able to separate these two components and to focus attention on the second. An application of this consideration can be found in the performance measurement system of Bently-Nevada of Minden, Nevada. In this system, the operator faced by a late order is evaluated on two objectives: order lateness and percentage of orders completed within the planned operation lead time. The operator is not penalized for failing to meet the late order's due date as long as he is able to complete the order within the planned operation lead time.

8. *Differentiate between "controllable" and "uncontrollable" problems.* The performance measures should monitor the ability of the user to cope with controllable problems. It is only for such problems that the PAC system can realistically hold the operator accountable. A controllable problem is one that the operator can prevent or one to which the operator can effectively respond. A machine breakdown due to poor preventive maintenance is an example of a controllable problem. The operator could have avoided the breakdown by doing the required maintenance. Longer processing times

due to brittle castings are an example of an uncontrollable problem. The responsibility for the castings lies with the vendor, not the operator.

9. *Facilitate comparisons.* The performance measures should facilitate comparison of performance across either work centers or departments. They should clearly identify the areas (work centers or departments) that have done a good job. They should also promote communications between areas so that the experiences of the good performers can be drawn on to help those experiencing problems. Finally, they should encourage competition among areas and thus foster the drive to do better.

10. *Reviewed and revised regularly.* As the firm and its requirements for success change over time, so should the performance measures. If the performance measures do not change, they lose their validity.

11. *Provide tough but realistic goals.* The performance measures should reflect objectives that force the user to extend himself and to work to the best of his ability. The objectives should present the user with a challenge, but one that is never beyond his grasp. Otherwise, the performance measures and the underlying objectives lose their validity in the eyes of the user.

12. *Adequate education for the users.* The users of the performance measures should be trained to understand what the measures are, why they are employed, what they mean, and how they are calculated. Such training leads to a better understanding of the performance measures.

13. *Emphasize the positive aspects of the performance measures.* The performance measures should not be regarded as means by which supervisors can punish poor performance. Instead, these measures should be seen as means by which the users can identify for themselves how they are doing. Furthermore, these measures provide important means by which the users can identify and correct any problems at an early stage. In short, the performance measures should be presented as being an aid, not a deterrence, to the users.

This list of considerations is not exhaustive. However, it does identify some very important factors that have a significant impact on the overall quality of the performance measures used.


## PAC ACTIVITIES—A SUMMARY

The information presented in this book has examined in some detail the methods and procedures by which the various PAC activities are carried out in an effective PAC system. As is evident from the preceding discussion, many factors must be considered in structuring such a system. An effective PAC system has certain characteristics. The most important of these characteristics are:

1. *Timely Information Flow.* There is an information flow that permits appropriate planning execution and feedback for replanning. The information flow takes place in daily or shorter time periods (such as with continuous real-time updating).
2. *Data Integrity.* The manufacturing data base used by the PAC system is characterized by:
   *a.* Accurate data and information.
   *b.* Computerized edits, preferably done on a real-time basis.
   *c.* A common source of input for accountability.
   *d.* An appropriate feedback mechanism.
3. *System Transparency.* The effective PAC system is transparent. That is, it is easy to use, easy to understand, and credible to all of the personnel involved.
4. *Simple Procedures.* The effective PAC system makes extensive use of simple procedures. Such procedures have been found to produce the best results. Simple procedures possess the following characteristics:
   *a.* They are formal but fast, allowing personnel the flexibility to react to changing company objectives.
   *b.* They are standard and documented.
   *c.* They result in greater knowledgeability regarding procedures among the personnel who use them.
5. *Accountability.* The effective PAC system places a high premium on accountability. Within such a system, responsibility and accountability are well defined, well doc-

umented, and understood by all of the personnel involved. Furthermore, the measures used in evaluating shop floor personnel and the performance of the PAC system reflect corporate objectives.

6. *Communication.* There is constant communication among all systems, personnel, and functional levels.

7. *Adequate Capacity.* The manufacturing planning system releases to the PAC system schedules for which it has provided adequate capacity. One of the major responsibilities of the PAC system is to manage the shop floor resources that it obtains from the manufacturing planning system.

8. *Effective Leadership.* In the effective PAC system, the leadership is characterized by:
   *a.* Positive attitudes.
   *b.* Continual promotion of effective changes within the system.
   *c.* An emphasis on a "can do" attitude.
   *d.* A continual striving to be a little better daily.

These characteristics of the effective PAC system are essentially derived from four major elements, which are graphically summarized in Figure 21. The elements are:

1. *People.* The computer systems of the effective PAC system are designed to be used by people. The success of the PAC system depends extensively on human beings. It is people who make the PAC system work; it is also people who bring to the PAC system much of the operating detail to which the system does not have access. The effective PAC system is therefore easy to use and understand. It is designed to make the maximum use of the detailed information and insights possessed by shop floor personnel.

2. *Accountability.* Someone is held accountable for every action taken in the PAC system. Accountability ensures that all PAC personnel take their responsibilities seriously. It also ensures that they view the actions indicated by the PAC computer systems as only recommendations. The PAC people are expected to evaluate selves the implications of these recommendations before accepting and acting on them. After all, should something go

---

**FIGURE 21**  Keys to
Effective PAC

---

**P**eople

**A**ccountability

**C**apacity

**S**ystems

---

wrong, the user, not the computer, will be held responsible. Finally, accountability is the price that the PAC people pay in return for this increased power within the PAC system.

3. *Capacity.* The effective PAC system is a resource manager. It is given the task of managing the shop floor resources given to it by the manufacturing planning system. Without adequate capacity, the PAC system cannot be expected to carry out the plans assigned to it by the planning system. It does not have the ability or the authority to make up any shortfalls in capacity. That ability and authority belong to the manufacturing planning system alone. Consequently, the manufacturing planning system is held responsible for generating feasible plans (i.e., plans for which there is enough capacity); the PAC system is then responsible for carrying out the plans and for improving efficiency (by taking advantage of similarities in setups or components or by assigning orders to the machines and people that are best able to process them).

4. *Systems.* The effective PAC system gives the users the support they need. Extensive computer systems are provided for several reasons. They relieve the users of the need to engage in such routine activities as recording data and reconciling balances. They identify potential shop floor problems by flagging out-of-tolerance situations. They keep users informed of changes taking place in the PAC system. Finally, they advance possible solutions

and offer users the ability to evaluate these solutions through simulation ("what if") analysis. In these ways, computer systems support the decision-making activities of PAC personnel by providing them with the tools they need.

Irrespective of the firm or the manufacturing setting, these four elements are essential to the development and presence of an effective PAC system. The guidelines provided in this book are intended to help the reader develop such a system.

# CHAPTER TEN

# Production Activity Control:
# Guidelines for Interfacing
# and Implementation

In the preceding chapters of this book, the primary focus has been on the activities of effective PAC. This focus represents a natural and logical method of thinking about production activity control. However, this focus is limited because it ignores two important topics that are not activity-related:

1. The interrelationships that exist between the PAC system and the rest of the firm.
2. The key steps in the "successful" implementation process.

These two topics must be examined in any complete treatment of effective PAC. They are the major subject of this final chapter.

## INTERFACING THE PAC SYSTEM WITH THE REST OF THE FIRM

The PAC system does not exist in isolation. It operates as a subsystem within the manufacturing system. It also operates as a subsystem within the entire corporate system. As a result, the PAC system is affected by decisions taken within these larger systems. Actions and decisions taken within the PAC system, in

**145**

turn, affect these larger systems. Therefore, the effective management of PAC depends, to a large extent, on how it is interfaced
with these larger systems and with certain functional areas within
them. Of special interest to the PAC system are the linkages
between PAC and:

Marketing/sales
Engineering
Manufacturing engineering
Finance/cost accounting
Quality assurance
Purchasing.

## Marketing/Sales and PAC

Marketing/sales and PAC are closely linked by the very nature of
their activities. PAC depends on marketing to communicate the
true priorities of orders, while marketing depends on PAC both
to fill the orders that marketing requires and to communicate the
actual status of orders. The linkages between marketing/sales
and PAC can be improved by focusing on the following areas:

- *Demand Management.* Marketing needs to communicate
  to PAC any activities (current or in the near future) that
  will affect product demand. Of particular interest to PAC
  are promotions. Promotions are a major source of uncertainty for PAC personnel, for they can change the nature
  of demand (i.e., quantity and mix) very quickly and without warning. The marketing department must keep PAC
  personnel (especially those involved in order review/re-
  lease and detailed scheduling) aware of when promotions
  are to be run and of what kinds of promotion are being
  used (e.g., "two for one" versus "cents off"). PAC personnel can then plan for the promotions and take the
  appropriate actions. Such actions might include the early
  release of promotion-bound orders or the addition of extra capacity (through overtime, second shifts, or subcontracting).
- *Production Plan.* The production plan communicates to
  the PAC system the long-term sales goals (as well as the
  patterns over time of these goals). It also informs PAC

personnel of the shop floor's responsibilities to the production plan. Such information can be used, for example, to identify potential periods of high demand (which may require moving workers around to provide the necessary capacity).

- *Efficiencies.* Information on efficiencies, provided by the PAC system, tells marketing/sales of the extent to which the load, as measured in standard hours, is an adequate indication of the capabilities of the shop floor. Under conditions where efficiencies are dropping, marketing may choose to reduce its load on the shop floor (until the problems causing the lower efficiencies have been cleared up).

- *Utilization.* Like efficiency, utilization is an indication of the capabilities of the shop floor. Information on utilization can be used to influence marketing plans. For example, low utilization may indicate to marketing that this is a good time for a promotion. High utilization may indicate that marketing should be very careful in selecting orders. Only orders for which capacity is available should be accepted. Otherwise, marketing may be faced by lengthening lead times and missed due dates.

- *Material Availability.* Like utilization, material availability indicates shop floor capabilities. For example, if non-allocated material is available for a particular order, marketing can arrange for the delivery of that order in less than the normal lead time.

- *Master Scheduling (Material and Capacity).* The master schedule indicates the amount of orders that the PAC system can be expected to process over a given period of time. This information can be seen as constraining marketing, since it indicates the potential upper limit on the number of new orders that the PAC system can be expected to process.

- *Customer Order Promising.* The customer order promising indicates to the shop floor which orders are intended for customers versus which orders are intended for stock replenishment. This information plays a key role in the dispatching process of the PAC system.

- *Customer Service Levels (Backlogs).* The extent of order backlogs indicates to marketing the capability of the PAC system to accept more orders. As backlogs increase, the capability of the PAC system to accept more orders and to process these orders within the normally quoted lead times decreases. If these backlogs are held off the shop floor by marketing, they indicate to PAC personnel the amount of work expected in future periods.

- *Customer Order Lead Times.* Information on customer order lead times, generated by the PAC system, indicates to marketing the lead times that should be considered in responding to customer orders.

### Engineering and PAC

It is the product and its design and representation that encourage close cooperation between engineering and the PAC system. After all, engineering is responsible for the design of the product, while the PAC system is a major user of the information generated by engineering. The following are crucial to ensuring the development and maintenance of an effective interrelationship between engineering and PAC:

- *Bill of Material Structuring.* Both engineering and the PAC system use the same manufacturing information. Both are interested in the development and use of a single accurate bill of materials. This concern provides a natural basis for linking these two systems. The bills of materials used by PAC personnel must be identical to the ones developed by engineering. Any errors or problems in these bills that are identified on the shop floor must be fed back to engineering and corrected. Finally, the pressure toward a single, common bill is not confined to PAC and engineering. Most firms now require that there be only one bill of material for every item.
- *Product Standardization.* The standardization of products should never be undertaken by engineering alone (especially in the case of products that are currently being produced by the firm). PAC personnel can contribute to this task by drawing on their experiences with the products. Product standardization should therefore be dealt with by a committee in which PAC personnel have a role.

- *Engineering Changes.* Engineering change notices (ECNs) are needed to adjust the bill of materials for changes resulting from such factors as product changes, safety considerations, and errors in documentation. The PAC system is both affected by and a source of these changes. ECNs can be produced by shop personnel in response to documentation errors and problems with machine utilization. PAC personnel should therefore be included in any committee dealing with ECNs.
- *BOM Maintenance.* For the reasons identified in connection with product standardization and engineering changes, the responsibility for maintaining the bill of materials must be jointly shared by the PAC system and engineering.
- *Prototype Planning.* New products should be planned by means of prototype committees in which such groups as engineering, PAC, finance, and purchasing are brought together. Engineering understands the design issues regarding the new product, while PAC personnel understand the modifications that must be made if the new product is to be readily produced on the shop floor.
- *Computer-Aided Design.* The designs generated by the CAD process (usually under the control of engineering) should be submitted to the PAC system for review and suggestions. These inputs will reflect the insights and experiences of PAC personnel.

## Finance/Cost Accounting and PAC

The data generated by the finance and cost accounting departments are coming to play an increasingly important role in the operation of the PAC system. PAC decisions are now being evaluated in terms of their cost implications. Consequently, representatives from the PAC system should be given the opportunity to express the concerns of the PAC system in discussions with finance/cost accounting personnel on such issues as:

Standard cost buildups.
Labor reporting and auditing.
Cycle counting and auditing.
Make versus buy analysis.

Cost centers versus profit centers (whether a department or work center should be treated as a cost center or as a profit center and the implications of this decision for PAC personnel).

Analysis of actual versus standard costs.

Variance analysis.

Budget analysis.

Traditionally, finance/cost accounting and the PAC system have used different data bases. However, this situation is changing. Since the data base needed by the PAC system is essentially the same as that needed by finance and manufacturing cost control, the two data bases have been merged in some firms. This merger of data bases is yet another factor forcing closer linkages between these two systems.[1]

The interface between finance/cost accounting and the PAC system typically tends to be very difficult to establish in practice. These two systems tend to measure performance in different terms. They tend to view the production process differently. In some instances, personnel from these systems may not see the need for developing such interfaces. However, these interfaces must be developed. Forcing a constant interaction between the two systems results in important cross-education. Finance/cost accounting begins to understand the operation of the shop floor and its capabilities and limitations. PAC personnel, on the other hand, develop an understanding of the financial and cost accounting measures and their impact on the operation of the PAC system. Developing an interface between finance/cost accounting and the PAC system reduces friction and conflict.

## Quality Assurance and PAC

Quality assurance is closely tied to PAC. The actions taken by quality assurance on an ongoing basis have a significant impact on the operation of the PAC system. For example, the quality

---

[1]For a further discussion of the issues involved in this merger of data bases, see J. Lundemann, "Integrating Inventory Control and the Cost Accounting System," *American Production and Inventory Control Society 26th Annual Conference Proceedings,* New Orleans, 1983, pp. 436–41.

standards set and maintained for incoming vendor-supplied parts can affect the processing times and the levels of scrap encountered on the shop floor. Quality assurance determines the quality standards used by PAC personnel when monitoring the flow of work on the shop floor. In turn, quality assurance depends on PAC personnel to implement the quality standards. Furthermore, quality assurance relies on feedback from the shop floor pertaining to the appropriateness of the standards being used, the extent to which vendor standards are being met, and quality-related problems that should be monitored. The linkage between quality assurance and the PAC system is most effectively maintained by focusing on:

- *In-Process Inspection.* For in-process inspection to be carried out effectively, the standards set by quality assurance must be stated in unambiguous and simple terms. Furthermore, quality assurance must ensure that the shop floor personnel understand the standards and are adequately trained in their application. The PAC system, on the other hand, must not only carry out in-process inspection on a continuous basis but must also monitor the standards being used. It must report back to quality assurance any problems with standards as promptly as possible. The process of setting standards and carrying them out during in-process inspection should be an ongoing process in which both systems participate.
- *Quality Assurance in Vendors.* Quality assurance, in cooperation with purchasing, provides the PAC system with a list of vendors that can meet the firm's quality standards; the PAC system identifies any quality problems with these vendors (which may require corrective action from quality assurance).
- *Scrap and Audits/Salvage and Audits.* The PAC system should not only collect data on scrap and salvage but should also identify reasons for these problems. This information can be drawn on by quality assurance to identify corrective actions that can be taken to resolve the problems (e.g., change vendors or materials).
- *Final Inspection.*
- *Quality History Programs.*

## Manufacturing Engineering and PAC

While the product links engineering to the PAC system, it is the process that ties manufacturing engineering to the PAC system. One objective of this linkage is to ensure that the manufacturing data used and developed by manufacturing engineering is the same as the manufacturing data used on the shop floor. In addition, both manufacturing engineering and the PAC system are interested in improving the efficiency of the manufacturing process. The process of improving efficiency cannot be realistically assigned to one group alone. Instead, it is a cooperative effort. Manufacturing engineering provides design expertise. The PAC system identifies areas that are candidates for improvement and suggests potential improvements in the manufacturing process. The ties between manufacturing engineering and the PAC system are maintained in numerous ways:

Capacity (output) analysis.
Efficiencies.
Utilization.
Routing maintenance.
Shop order maintenance.
Lead time maintenance.
Make versus buy analysis.
Capital equipment analysis.
Prototype planning.
Lot sizing analysis.
Productivity improvement programs.
Computer-aided manufacturing (CAM).

## Purchasing and PAC

Purchasing and the PAC system are linked by their concern over the flow of components coming in from vendors. Purchasing is responsible for securing adequate sources that can provide needed components at the times required. The PAC system, in turn, is responsible for identifying problems involving vendors (e.g., quality, on-time delivery, quantity) and for feeding this information back to purchasing. Purchasing must rely on this feedback from the users (in this case manufacturing in general and the PAC system specifically) when evaluating its vendors.

The relationship between purchasing and the PAC system is maintained by:

Schedule receipt versus load analysis.
Make versus buy analysis.
Prototype planning.
Lot size analysis.
Count assured vendor.
Vendor capacity forecasts.
Vendor product improvement programs.

## Interfacing PAC with the Rest of the Firm—Summary Comments

As pointed out at the start of this section, the PAC system does not operate in isolation. Many of the problems encountered by PAC personnel are best resolved by working with other functions within the firm. Many of the decisions made within the PAC system are best made jointly. Much of the information generated by the PAC system is of interest to other areas in the firm. Consequently, getting the greatest benefits from the PAC system requires not only that the PAC activities be structured "correctly" but also that the PAC system be linked to other functional groups.

This section has identified some of the more important linkages that can ensure the effective integration of the PAC system.

## IMPLEMENTING PAC: A CHECKLIST

To gain the benefits offered by an effective PAC system, such a system must first be put in place. These benefits cannot be achieved overnight. Ensuring that the prerequisites for an effective PAC system are present and that the PAC activities are correctly structured requires time, money, and the cooperation of numerous groups within the firm (both inside and outside the manufacturing system).

The following is a general checklist of the factors that should be considered when undertaking the implementation of a PAC system:

1. *Adequate Training and Education.* A key first step in any implementation process is training and education. These two activities should be directed both downward to the shop floor personnel and upward to top management. The support and understanding of both levels are required for the successful implementation of the PAC system. For the shop floor personnel, training and education should cover:
    a. Foreman understanding of the dispatching list and the formal capacity planning systems (such as CRP).
    b. Remedial action steps when priorities cannot be followed.
    c. Pilot simulation of the operation of the PAC system on the computer.

    For top management, training and education should cover:
    a. A general understanding operation and objectives of the PAC system.
    b. Identification of the capabilities and limitations of the PAC system and the importance of adequate capacity and material planning system to the operation of PAC.
    c. The linkages tying the PAC system to the rest of the firm.
    d. An understanding of the key reports used by shop floor personnel.
    e. Remedial action steps when priorities cannot be satisfied.
    f. Expected costs, benefits, and implementation time frame.
2. *Discipline.* Key to the successful implementation of any PAC system is discipline. If the system is to work as planned, discipline must be based on:
    a. Timely data collection.
    b. The elimination of "cherry picking" shop orders on the dispatch list.
    c. Union understanding of and compliance with PAC procedures. This includes the elimination of such undesirable procedures as the banking of labor.
    d. Timely move and labor transactions.

3. *Data Base Requirements.* The successful implementation of the PAC system is closely tied to the overall quality of the manufacturing data base. An acceptable data base consists of:

   *a.* Accurate standard routings, with setup times based on either engineered standards or estimates and run times that are either engineered standards or estimates.

   *b.* Alternative routings.

   *c.* Work center definition with standard queue times, direct labor and machine capacity, move times, shifts worked, standard and current costs for labor, setup and burden (fixed plus variable), queue compression factors, person to machine conversion factors, and factors to calculate capacity if appropriate.

   *d.* Tooling with the capability to:

      (1) Call out tools by operation maintained through a tool bill of material.

      (2) Tool kit if tools are too numerous to list by operation.

      (3) Generate a tool pick list by shop order with tools listed by operation number.

4. *Lead Times.* Planned manufacturing lead times are important to any PAC system. They are used in calculating order priorities and in determining "recommended" order release and due dates. These lead time values should therefore be checked for reasonableness.

5. *Top-Management Commitment.* The successful implementation of a PAC system requires the continued support and commitment of top management. The level of top-management commitment and support must be continually monitored.

6. *Software.* Functional software with source code should be available for modification. Very few PAC systems can be implemented without some sort of software modification.

7. *Planning System.* A completely successful planning system should be implemented. This system should consist of production planning, master production scheduling, rough cut capacity planning, a formal material planning

system (such as MRP), and a formal capacity planning system (such as CRP).

These are some of the major points that should always be kept in mind during the implementation of a PAC system. However, implementation is only the first step in the process of developing and maintaining an effective PAC system. Once implemented, the system must constantly be monitored and its operation fine-tuned.

# References

1. "Voice Recognition—Back Again and Better," *Modern Materials Handling,* April 6, 1983, pp. 52-55.

2. J. Browne, J. E. Boon, and B. J. Davies, "Job Shop Control," *International Journal of Production Research* 19, no. 6 (1981), pp. 633-43.

3. D. W. Fogarty and T. R. Hoffmann, *Production and Inventory Management* (Cincinnati: South-Western Publishing, 1983).

4. J. H. Greene, *Production and Inventory Control: Systems and Decisions* (Homewood, Ill.: Richard D. Irwin, 1974).

5. IBM, "Chapter 1: Engineering and Production," in *Communications Oriented Production Information and Control System,* vol. 2 (White Plains, N.Y.: IBM Technical Publications Department, 1972).

6. IBM, "Chapter 6: Manufacturing Activity Planning," in *Communications Oriented Production Information and Control System,* vol. 5 (White Plains, N.Y.: IBM Technical Publications Department, 1972).

7. IBM, "Chapter 7: Order Release," in *Communications Oriented Production Information and Control System,* vol. 5 (White Plains, N.Y.: IBM Technical Publications Department, 1972).

8. IBM, "Chapter 8: Plant Monitoring and Control," in *Communications Oriented Production Information and Control System,* vol. 6 (White Plains, N.Y.: IBM Technical Publications Department, 1972).

9. IBM, "Chapter 9: Plant Maintenance," in *Communications Oriented Production Information and Control System,* vol. 6 (White Plains, N.Y.: IBM Technical Publications Department, 1972).

10. J. Lundemann, "Integrating Inventory Control and the Cost Accounting System," *American Production and Inventory Control 26th Annual Conference Proceedings,* New Orleans, 1983.

11. S. A. Melnyk, P. L. Carter, D. M. Dilts, and D. M. Lyth, *Shop Floor Control* (Homewood, Ill.: Dow Jones-Irwin, 1985).

12. Milwaukee APICS Chapter, *APICS Training Aid: Shop Floor Control* (Washington, D.C.: American Production and Inventory Control Society, 1973).

13. J. A. Orlicky, *Material Requirements Planning* (New York: McGraw-Hill, 1975).

14. A. Paradiso, "Bar Coding: A Brief Introduction," *Production and Inventory Management Review* 2, no. 6 (June 1982), pp. 16–19.

15. T. F. Wallace, ed., *APICS Dictionary,* 4th ed. (Washington, D.C.: American Production and Inventory Control Society, 1980).

16. O. W. Wight, "Input/Output Control: A Real Handle on Lead Time," *Production and Inventory Management* 11, no. 3 (1970), pp. 9–30.

# Glossary of
# Key Production Activity Control Terms

The following terms are important to a clear understanding of PAC. These terms have been used in the guide and are defined in this section for clarification.

**Automated Identification.** A broad term used to describe any information gathering procedure in which information is encoded in a form that can be transmitted and recorded using an electronic device. There are four major forms of automated identification procedures: bar coding, optical character recognition, magnetic strips, and voice recording. (See *Bar Code; Optical Character Recognition; Magnetic Strips.*)

**Automation.** The technology concerned with the application of complex mechanical, electrical, electronic, and computer-based systems in the operation and control of production. This technology includes (1) automatic machine tools for processing parts, (2) automatic material handling systems, (3) automatic assembly machines, (4) continuous-flow processes, (5) feedback control systems, (6) computer process control systems, and (7) computerized systems for data collection, planning, and decision making to support manufacturing activities (Groover, 1980, pp. 3–4).

**Backward Scheduling.** A form of scheduling (see *Scheduling*) that begins with the order due date and proceeds backward through the various required operations to arrive at the latest start date for the order.

**Bar Code.** An array of rectangular bars and spaces arranged in a predetermined pattern to represent characters for machine reading.

**Breakdown Maintenance.** See *Maintenance, Breakdown.*

**Capacity.** The capability of a facility to process a workload in a given period of time. Typically, the workload processed is measured in terms of an aggregate unit of measurement such as standard hours.

**Capacity Control.** The process of measuring production output and comparing it with the level of planned output, as indicated by a formal capacity planning system such as capacity requirements planning (see *Capacity Requirements Planning*), determining whether the variance exceeds preestablished limits, and taking the appropriate corrective action to get back to plan if the limits are exceeded (*APICS Dictionary,* 1980, p. 4). Typically, the adjustments are made by means of short-term changes in capacity.

**Capacity Evaluation.** A part of the order release activity in production activity control (see *Order Release*). During capacity evaluation, the capacity required by the shop order is compared with the capacity available in the system. If the available capacity is inadequate, the release of the order may be delayed until the required capacity becomes available.

**Capacity Planning.** See *Capacity Requirements Planning.*

**Capacity Requirements Planning.** Also referred to as "CRP." The function of establishing, measuring, and adjusting limits or levels of capacity that are consistent with a production plan. In this context, capacity requirements planning is the process of determining what quantity of labor and machine resources is required to accomplish the tasks of production (*APICS Dictionary,* 1980, p. 4).

**Capacity Utilization.** See *Utilization.*

**Cellular Layout.** As contrasted to the functional layout (see *Functional Layout*), a physical rearrangement of the shop floor in which the various machines are grouped into manufacturing cells (see *Manufacturing Cell*). A physical implementation of cellular manufacturing (see *Cellular Manufacturing*).

**Cellular Manufacturing.** The organization of a small group of workers and machines in a repetitive production flow layout to manufacture a group of similar items. It achieves economies due to the modified equipment dedicated to the group, special tooling, reduced setup and run time, reduced material handling, shorter throughput time, and reduced WIP (Fogarty and Hoffmann, 1983, p. 471).

**Closed Loop Material Requirements Planning.** Also referred to as "closed loop MRP." A system built around material requirements planning (see *Material Requirements Planning*) that includes the additional production-oriented planning functions of production planning, master production scheduling, and capacity requirements planning. Once the planning phase has been completed and the plans have been accepted as realistic and attainable, the execution functions (and production activity control) come into play. The term *closed loop* implies that each of these elements is included in the overall system and that there is feedback from each lower level of the system to the higher levels in order to ensure that the plans are kept valid at all times (*APICS Dictionary,* 1980, p. 5).

**Closed Loop MRP.**  See *Closed Loop Material Requirements Planning.*

**Continuous Manufacturing.**  A major classification of production involving the high-volume production of a nondiscrete item (e.g., petroleum) in a process characterized by a sequence of operations common to most items, short lead times, and very small queues.

**Control.**  Also referred to as "capacity control." Part of the fourth major phase of production activity control. Control involves the short-term adjustment of shop floor capacity in order to compensate for difficulties being experienced by the out-of-control order (i.e., a shop order whose actual progress is not sufficiently close to its planned progress).

**Control/Feedback.**  The fourth major phase of production activity control. This phase involves the actions undertaken by management at various levels of the firm in controlling out-of-control shop orders.

**CPM.**  See *Critical Path Method.*

**Critical Path Method.**  Also referred to as "CPM." A network planning technique used in scheduling and controlling the various activities of a project. Critical path method shows the sequence of each activity and its associated time. This enables management to determine the latest and earliest start date for each activity, the latest and earliest finish date for each activity, and the critical path for the entire project. The critical path identifies the elements that actually constrain the total time for the project. The project's minimum completion time is determined by the critical path. (See *Project Evaluation and Review Technique.*)

**Critical Ratio Rule.**  Also referred to as "CRR." The critical ratio rule is a priority rule that determines an order's priority by dividing the time remaining to the order due date by the expected remaining processing time. The remaining processing time may or may not include an allowance for queue time. The result is a ratio. Typically, a ratio of less than 1.0 indicates that the order is behind schedule, a ratio greater than 1.0 indicates that the order is ahead of schedule, and a ratio of 1.0 indicates that the order is on schedule. (See *Dispatching Rule.*)

**CRP.**  See *Capacity Requirements Planning.*

**CRR.**  See *Critical Ratio Rule.*

**Customer Service Level.** A measure of the availability of items to the customer.

**Data Base, Manufacturing.** See *Manufacturing Data Base.*

**Data Collection/Monitoring.** The third major phase of production activity control. This phase consists of all the activities involving the collection of information pertaining to the progress of shop orders as they move through the various stages of their routing and the comparison of this information against standards. The purpose of the comparison is to identify orders that may require intervention by the PAC personnel.

**Dependent Priority.** Recognizing that the priority of an order depends on the availability, or lack of availability, of other inventory items at the time of order completion (Orlicky, 1975, pp. 146–47). Dependent priority is broken down into two categories: horizontal dependency and vertical dependency. (See *Horizontal Dependency; Vertical Dependency.*)

**Detailed Scheduling.** The second major stage of production activity control. Detailed assignment consists of the activities that formally match the supply of shop floor resources (labor, machines, inventory, and tools) to the demands placed on these resources. The demands come from competing orders, scheduled preventive maintenance, and scheduled downtime. The assignments are stated in terms that identify (1) which resources are to be assigned, (2) the quantity of resources to be assigned, (3) the time at which the resources are to be assigned, (4) the location from which the resources are to be drawn, and (5) the priority in which the various competing demands are to gain access to the appropriate resources. (Compare *Maintenance, Preventive.*)

**Discrete Batch Manufacturing.** Also referred to as "job shop manufacturing." A classification of production processes that involves the production of discrete units in small batches. These batches need not follow the same sequence of operations (in contrast with continuous or repetitive manufacturing). Lead time tends to be relatively long due to large queues.

**Dispatch List.** A listing of manufacturing orders in priority sequence according to the dispatching rules. The dispatch list, which is usually communicated to the manufacturing floor via hard copy or CRT display, contains detailed information on priority, location, quantity, and the capacity requirements of the manufacturing order by operation. Dispatch lists are normally generated daily and oriented by work center (*APICS Dictionary,* 1980, pp. 8–9). (Compare *Dispatching Rule.*)

**Dispatcher.** A shop floor employee responsible for determining the sequence in which orders are to be processed through the various work centers.

**Dispatching.** The selection and sequencing of jobs to be run at individual work centers and the authorization or assignment of work to be done (*APICS Dictionary,* 1980, p. 8).

**Dispatching Rule.**   The logic or predetermined set of steps used when assigning priorities to jobs waiting at a given work center (*APICS Dictionary,* 1980, p. 8).

**Due Date.**   The latest time at which an order is to complete a prespecified set of actions and be made available to the planning system for subsequent actions. The due date can be stated as either an operation or order due date. (See *Operation Due Date; Order Due Date.*)

**Earliest Due Date.**   Also referred to as "EDD." A dispatching rule that sequences orders waiting in a queue according to order due date. The job with the lowest order due date is given the highest priority in that queue, while the job with the highest order due date is given the lowest priority. (See *Dispatching Rule; Order Due Date.*)

**Earliest Operation Due Date.**   Also referred to as "EODD." A dispatching rule that sequences orders waiting in a queue according to operation due date. The job with the lowest operation due date is assigned the highest priority in that queue, while the job with the highest operation due date is given the lowest priority. (See *Dispatching Rule; Operation Due Date.*)

**EDD.**   See *Earliest Due Date.*

**EODD.**   See *Earliest Operation Due Date.*

**Exception Reporting.**   A formal report produced by the production activity control system that relates information concerning shop floor difficulties to the managers responsible for resolving the difficulties. Produced during the control/feedback phase of production activity control (see *Control/Feedback*).

**Expediting.**   All of the activities that are undertaken by shop floor personnel to ensure that critically needed parts and orders are available in time to meet delivery commitments. The most significant expediting activities include interoperation time reduction, overlapping and operation splitting, lot splitting, and temporary augmentation of shop floor capacity.

**FCFS.**   See *First Come, First Served.*

**Feedback.**   An activity of the control/feedback stage of production activity control (see *Control/Feedback*). Feedback is the process of relating information regarding the progress of shop orders (with special emphasis on those considered out of control) to the planning system. The planning system may choose to evaluate alternatives to correct current problems. The corrective actions introduced frequently affect either the demands placed on the shop floor or the demand for the problem orders.

**FIFO.** First in, First Out. See *First Come, First Served.*

**Finite Loading.** Putting an amount of work into a department or work center that is equal to or less than its capacity in any period.

**First Come, First Served.** A dispatching rule that sequences jobs in the same order as they arrive. Also referred to as "FCFS" and "FIFO" [first in, first out]. (See *Dispatching Rule.*)

**First In, First Out.** See *First Come, First Served.*

**Forced Release.** A shorted order that is released to the shop floor in cases where off-standard material can be substituted or the missing components are expected to arrive before they are needed by the order. (See *Shorted Order.*)

**Forward Scheduling.** A form of scheduling (see *Scheduling*) that begins with a known start date for the first operation and proceeds from that operation until the last required operation. The earliest completion date for the order can be determined by forward scheduling.

**Functional Layout.** A physical arrangement of the shop floor in which the various machines are grouped together based on the similarity of the function performed. A contrast to the cellular layout (see *Cellular Layout*).

**Gateway Work Center.** A work center in which work begins. Typically, a gateway work center is one through which most of the orders released to the shop floor must begin.

**Group Technology.** A systematic methodology where component similarity is used to form part families, plan common production processes, and establish manufacturing cells so that economic benefits are achieved (Levulis, 1980, p. 267).

**Horizontal Dependency.** A type of dependent priority. Horizontal dependency is the realization that the priority of any component order is affected by the progress of the other components needed in the parent assembly. If one or more of these component orders are unavailable (due to such problems as excessive scrap or machine breakdown), the priority of the other orders should be altered, since they will not be needed on the original due date. (See *Dependent Priority.*)

**Infinite Loading.** Determining the amount of work that has to be performed in a work center regardless of the capacity available to perform this work. Used to the determine the match with capacity demands and capacity availability. (See *Capacity Requirements Planning.*)

**Input/Output Control.** A technique for capacity control in which actual output from a work center is compared with the planned output developed by a formal capacity planning system such as capacity requirements planning. The input is also monitored to see whether it corresponds with plans (*APICS Dictionary,* 1980, p. 13). Input/output control enables the user to identify whether the production problems being experienced at a certain work center are the result of problems in processing (capacity imbalances) or problems in the rate of order input, or both.

**Input/Output Planning.**  A capacity planning technique that plans input and output to a plant or department, with differences between input and output affecting work-in-process inventory and lead time (Fogarty and Hoffmann, 1983, p. 681).

**Interactive Scheduling.**  A form of scheduling in which the order in which jobs are released or processed is determined in an iterative fashion involving the user and the computer. Typically, the user defines an initial schedule and feeds this schedule to the computer. The computer then determines the effects of the schedule and may suggest alternatives. Based on this feedback, the user formulates and inputs another schedule. This process continues until an acceptable schedule has been identified.

**Intermittent Production.**  See *Discrete Batch Manufacturing.*

**Interoperation Time.**  The time interval between the completion of one operation and the start of the next operation. Typically, interoperation time is the sum of queue time, preparation time, postoperation time, wait time, and transport time (IBM, Chapter 6, 1972, p. 22).

**Interoperation Time Reduction.**  A form of expediting that concentrates on reducing the amount of time that a "critical" order spends in interoperation time (i.e., waiting in queues or waiting for transportation to take it to the next operation). (See *Expediting.*)

**Job.**  See *Shop Order.*

**Job Shop Control.**  Another term for "production activity control." See *Production Activity Control* for definition.

**Job Shop Manufacturing.**  See *Discrete Batch Manufacturing.*

**Just-in-Time Manufacturing.**  A comprehensive system of production and inventory control that attempts to reduce the inventory and manufacturing waste within the production system to the lowest possible level by identifying and attacking all of the factors that cause such inventory to exist.

**Lead Time, Manufacturing.**  See *Manufacturing Lead Time.*

**Line Balancing.**  Reassigning and redesigning work done on an assembly line to make the work cycle times at all stations approximately equal (Hall, 1983, p. 19).

**Load.** The amount of scheduled work ahead of a manufacturing facility, usually expressed in hours of work or units of production.

**Load Leveling.** The procedure of shifting operations or order releases to smooth the demands placed on the personnel and machinery capacities of the shop floor over part or all of the relevant planning horizon.

**Lot Size.** Also referred to as an "order quantity." The quantity of a specific item that is ordered from either the plant or the vendor.

**Lot Sizing.** The process of determining lot sizes. Frequently involves the use of a lot sizing technique such as lot for lot or economic order quantity.

**Lot Splitting.** A form of expediting in which a critical order is broken up into several smaller lots. A sufficient quantity is then pushed ahead to satisfy the upcoming delivery requirements, while the remainder of the critical order is allowed to proceed normally (IBM, Chapter 6, 1972, p. 34). (See *Expediting.*)

**Machine Cell.** Another term for "manufacturing cell." See *Manufacturing Cell.*

**Magnetic Strip.** A form of automated identification (see *Automated Identification*). A relatively new procedure, the magnetic strip consists of magnetic stripes and characters that can be read by using hand-held wands or slot readers. The major advantage of magnetic strips is that they can encode information at much higher density than can either bar coding or optical characters.

**Maintenance, Breakdown.** Emergency maintenance, including diagnosis of the problem and repair of a machine or facility *after* a malfunction has occurred (IBM, Chapter 1, 1972, p. 13). A form of maintenance distinct from preventive maintenance (see *Maintenance, Preventive*).

**Maintenance, Preventive.** Maintenance work that is done at regular intervals. Preventive maintenance includes such routine operations as lubrication and inspection and such major jobs as the overhaul of a press (IBM, Chapter 1, 1972, p. 13). It describes any maintenance that is *not* triggered by the breakdown of a machine or facility.

**Manufacturing Activity Planning.** Another term for "production activity control." See *Production Activity Control.*

**Manufacturing Cell.** The manufacturing cell consists of all the machines required for the production of a part family. Most often the result of group technology (see *Group Technology*), the manufacturing cell can be found in a range of configurations. In its simplest form, the manufacturing cell can consist of only one machine. At the other end of the spectrum, the manufacturing cell can consist of a group of machines connected by a conveyor system.

**Manufacturing Data Base.**  A set of files (usually implemented on a computer system) that contain information of use to the manufacturing system. These files can be centrally located, or they can be dispersed, with each function controlling the files of direct interest to it.

**Manufacturing Data Sheet.**  See *Route Sheet.*

**Manufacturing Lead Time.**  The interval between the time an order is released from the planning system to the execution system and the time the order is completed and sent to inventory.

**Manufacturing Order.**  See *Shop Order.*

**Manufacturing Resource Planning.**  Also referred to as "MRP II." A method for the effective planning of all the resources of a manufacturing company. Ideally, this method addresses operational planning in units and financial planning in dollars, and it has a simulation capability to answer "what if" questions. It links together a variety of functions; business planning, production planning, capacity requirements planning, and the execution systems for capacity and priority. Outputs from these functions are integrated with financial reports, such as the business plan, the purchase commitment report, the shipping budget, and inventory projections. Manufacturing resource planning is a direct outgrowth and extension of MRP (material requirements planning) (*APICS Dictionary,* 1980, p. 16).

**MAP.**  See *Production Activity Control* for definition.

**Master Production Schedule.**  Also referred to as the "master schedule." The master production schedule is a statement of what the company expects to manufacture expressed in specific configurations, quantities, and dates. This schedule "drives" a formal material and priority planning system such as material requirements planning. It should not be confused with a sales forecast, which represents a statement of demand. The master production scheduler takes into account forecasts plus other important considerations (backlog, availability of material, availability of capacity, management policy and goals, etc.) prior to determining the best master production schedule (Berry, Vollmann, and Whybark, 1979, p. 180). The master production schedule influences the operation of the production activity control system since it determines both the total demand for capacity and the ultimate production priorities.

**Master Schedule.**  See *Master Production Schedule.*

**Material Checking.**  A major activity of the order review/release phase of production activity control (see *Order Review/Release*). Material checking is the checking of the inventory status and records of the components required by a shop order to ensure that these components will be available in sufficient quantity at the necessary time. Material checking determines whether lack of the needed component inventory will hinder the progress of the order through the shop.

**Material Requirements Planning.** A system that uses bills of material, inventory, planned lead times, open order data, and master production schedule information to calculate requirements for materials. The system makes recommendations to release replenishment orders for material and to reschedule open orders when due dates and need dates are not in phase. Originally seen as merely a better way to order inventory, material requirements planning is now viewed primarily as a scheduling technique—as a method for establishing and maintaining valid due dates on orders (*APICS Dictionary*, 1980, p. 18).

**MPS.** See *Master Production Schedule.*

**MRP.** See *Material Requirements Planning.*

**MRP II.** See *Manufacturing Resource Planning.*

**MS.** See *Master Production Schedule.*

**Need Date.** The date when net requirements for a component become positive. That is, the date when the combined coverage of on-hand inventory plus scheduled receipts are no longer sufficient to cover the gross requirements generated by that component's parents.

**Operation Due Date.** The latest date by which a job is to be completed at a given work center.

**Operation List.** See *Route Sheet.*

**Operation Splitting.** A method of expediting orders in which a critical order is performed in parallel on two or more machines or at two or more work stations. Usually requires the assignment of more personnel to the critical order. (See *Expediting.*)

**Operations Sequence.** See *Routing.*

**Optical Character Recognition.** A form of automated identification (see *Automated Identification*). Optical character recognition uses codes that can be read both by humans and by mechanical readers such as light pens and point-of-sale terminals.

**Order.** See *Shop Order.*

**Order Completion.** The process of closing out or disposing of an order. (See *Order Disposition.*)

**Order Disposition.** The fifth and final phase of production activity control. This phase describes all of the activities that the production activity control system must complete in order to relieve itself of responsibility for a shop order. Among these activities is the release of those shop floor resources assigned to but no longer needed by the shop order. On the completion of order disposition, the shop order can go into either inventory or scrap.

**Order Documentation.**  One of the activities undertaken during the order review/release phase of production activity control. Order documentation provides the shop order with the information that the shop floor needs to ensure the successful completion of the shop order. Typically, the information assigned by order documentation includes (1) order identification, (2) routings, (3) time standards, (4) material requirements, (5) tooling requirements, and (6) due dates (either operation or order). (See *Order Review/Release; Order Due Date; Operation Due Date.*)

**Order Due Date.**  The latest time by which a job is to be completed on the shop floor and made available to fulfill subsequent delivery commitments.

**Order Overlapping.**  See *Overlapping.*

**Order Release.**  See *Order Review/Release.*

**Order Review/Release.**  The first major phase of production activity control. The order review/release phase consists of the activities that must take place before an order released by the formal planning system can be allowed to enter the shop floor. The major activities of order review/release are (1) order documentation, (2) material checking, (3) capacity evaluation, and (4) load leveling. (See *Load Leveling; Order Documentation.*)

**Order Sequencing/Dispatching.**  The process of determining by means of a prespecified set of decision rules the sequence in which a facility is to process a number of shop orders. When processing these orders, order sequencing/dispatching is also responsible for the corresponding assignment of workers, tooling, and materials to the selected jobs. The order of resource assignment is consistent with a predetermined set of goals that the production activity control system attempts to satisfy (e.g., meeting due dates, reducing maximum lateness of orders).

**Out of Control.**  A term used to describe a shop order whose actual level of progress exceeds the preestablished limits set by a standard. Shop orders identified as being "out of control" are the objects of corrective actions taken by management.

**Overlapping.**  A method of expediting a critical job in which the next required operation is allowed to begin before the previous operation of the *entire* lot has been completed (IBM, Chapter 6, 1972, pp. 27–28). (See *Expediting.*)

**PAC.** See *Production Activity Control* for definition.

**Part Family.** A collection of parts that are similar either because their geometric shape and size are similar or because similar processing steps are required in their manufacture. The similarities of these parts are sufficient to merit their identification as members of the same part family (Groover, 1981, p. 539).

**Part Master File.** A component of the manufacturing data base. The part master file is part of the planning files. It records in one file all of the relevant data about a specific part. This file contains such information as part number, part description, scrap factors, and where used. A key source of data for production activity control.

**PERT.** See *Project Evaluation and Review Technique.*

**Picking.** The process of withdrawing from stock the components needed to make a product.

**Picking List.** A document used by shop floor personnel to pick or requisition component items from stores.

**Preparation Time.** The time during which an order is delayed prior to processing. Typically, preparation time is expressed as a percentage of the operation duration (i.e., the setup time plus the run time) (IBM, Glossary, 1972, p. 16). Preparation time is caused by some preparatory operation not in the routing, such as cleaning, heating, or marking out. A component of manufacturing lead time (see *Manufacturing Lead Time*).

**Preventive Maintenance.** See *Maintenance, Preventive.*

**Priority.** In a general sense, priority refers to the relative importance of jobs, that is, which jobs which should be worked on and when (Fogarty and Hoffmann, 1983, p. 693).

**Priority, Dependent.** See *Dependent Priority.*

**Priority Integrity.** Ensuring that the order priorities assigned actually reflect what must be produced (based on the master production schedule) and what can be produced (based on capacity availability) (Orlicky, 1975, p. 146).

**Priority Rule.** See *Dispatching Rule.*

**Priority Validity.** Maintaining the alignment between the due date and the indicated need date. In MRP, priority validity is considered a mechanical issue (Orlicky, 1975, p. 146).

**Process Routing.** See *Routing.*

**Production Activity Control.** Also referred to as "manufacturing activity planning" (MAP), "shop floor control" (SFC), and "job shop control." A major subsystem within the manufacturing system. Production activity control is that group of activities directly responsible for managing the transformation of planned orders (i.e., orders released to the shop floor by the planning system) into a set of outputs that conform to some set of prespecified evaluation criteria. Production activity control governs the *very short term* detailed planning, execution, and monitoring activities needed to control the flow of an order from the time that the order is released to the time that the order is filled and its disposition completed. The production activity control system is responsible for making the detailed and final allocation of labor, machine capacity, tooling, and materials to the various competing orders. It collects information on the shop floor activities involving the progress of various orders and the status of resources and makes this information available to the planning system. Production activity control consists of five major sets of activities: (1) order review/release, (2) detailed assignment, (3) data collection/monitoring, (4) control/feedback, and (5) order disposition. (See *Order Review/Release; Detailed Assignment; Data Collection/Monitoring; Control/Feedback; Order Disposition.*)

**Project.**  A major category of production. A project involves the production of a unique, one-of-a-kind product or service through the coordination of large amounts of resources that either have never before been organized into a single process or are brought together infrequently. Examples of project manufacturing include the construction of a transfer line, the development of a prototype, and the construction of a ship. Projects are most frequently managed by means of either PERT or CPM. (See *Critical Path Management; Project Evaluation and Review Technique.*)

**Project Evaluation and Review Technique.**  Also referred to as "PERT." A project planning technique similar to Critical Path Method. This technique includes a range of time estimates for the completion of each activity in the project. The range of estimates typically consists of a pessimistic, most likely, and optimistic time for each activity. These estimates are used in calculating the most likely completion time for the project along the critical path. (See *Critical Path Method.*)

**Pull System.**  (1) As applied in the context of production activity control, a system that is responsible for getting the right parts completed at the time of actual need. Examples of pull systems include expediting (see *Expediting*). (2) The production of items only as demanded for use or to replace those taken for use (Hall, 1983, p. 20).

**Push System.**  (1) As applied in the context of production activity control, a push system is one that launches orders onto the shop floor for completion. (See *Pull System.*) (2) The production of items at the times required by a given schedule planned in advance (Hall, 1983, p. 20).

**Queue.**  A waiting line of jobs available to go through an operation (i.e., process or work center) in the shop. (See *Queue Time.*)

**Queue Time.**  The amount of time that a job waits at a work center before it can gain control of the work center (i.e., until setup for the job has begun). In many production systems, queue time is the largest component of manufacturing lead time (see *Manufacturing Lead Time*).

**Repetitive Manufacturing.**  A classification of production involving the high-volume production of a discrete item that is either standard in form or made from standard options (e.g., automobiles) in a process with a sequence of operations common to most items, short lead times, and very small queues.

**Rescheduling.**  The changing of order or operation due dates, usually as a result of their being out of phase with when they are needed (Fogarty and Hoffmann, 1983, p. 696).

**Rework.**  The portion of a shop order that must go through additional steps in order to correct problems encountered on the shop floor. In rework, unlike salvage or scrap, the affected items of the order do not change identity.

**Route Sheet.**  Also referred to as a "process chart," "operation list," "operation sheet," "operation chart," and "manufacturing data sheet." A document that specifies the operations on a part and the sequence of operations, with alternative operations and routings wherever feasible. Other processing specifications that can be included on a route sheet are the material requirements (kind and quantity); the machine tolerances; the tools, jigs, and fixtures required; and the time allowance for each operation (*APICS Dictionary,* 1980, p. 24).

**Routing.**  Also called "operations sequence" or "process routing." A routing is a list of the steps required to complete the manufacture of a product. A routing describes what operations have to be done, where (i.e., department and work center) and by whom they have to be done, how much time is allowed for setup and run, and how much total elapsed time is allowed for each operation.

**Routing File.**  A component of the manufacturing data base. This file consists of a set of records for each manufactured part. It contains all of the information pertaining to the actions needed during the fabrication or assembly of an item. For each part, the routing file defines both the preferred sequence of production events and alternative sequences.

**Safety Capacity.**  That portion of the shop's total capacity, as measured in terms of tooling, personnel, and machine time, that is not used or allocated to production *on average.* The purpose of safety capacity is to enable the production activity control system to deal with unexpected changes either in the level of demand (i.e., increases in demand) or in capacity (i.e., decreases resulting from such factors as worker illness).

**Salvage.** The portion of a shop order that can no longer be completed in the form specified when the order was released. A portion of the order has experienced difficulties during processing that affect the final form taken by that portion. The affected portion can be processed into items of a form different from the one originally specified. These items can be used by the production system. An example of salvage is the recutting of a blemished 60-inch bolt of cloth into an unblemished 48-inch bolt of cloth.

**Scheduling.** (1) The sequencing or dispatching activity plus the determination of the lot size and the allocation of resources to complete the job. (2) The process of setting operation start dates and completion dates (due dates) for each order released to the shop floor. The purpose of assigning these dates is to indicate the operating constraints within which the order must operate if it is to be completed by its order due date. Scheduling can take the form of either forward scheduling or backward scheduling (see *Forward Scheduling; Backward Scheduling*).

**Scheduling, Backward.** See *Backward Scheduling.*

**Scheduling, Forward.** See *Forward Scheduling.*

**Scheduling, Interactive.** See *Interactive Scheduling.*

**Scrap.** Any portion of a shop order that is no longer usable by the manufacturing system.

**Sequencing.** Determining the order in which a manufacturing facility (e.g., work center) is to process a number of different jobs so as to achieve certain objectives (*APICS Dictionary,* 1980, p. 25).

**Setup Time.** The time required to prepare a machine or facility so that an order can be processed. Setup time is a major component of manufacturing lead time. The setup time can be either a standard time or an actual time. A standard setup time is the allowance provided for the setup of a machine or facility. An actual setup time is the time actually consumed by such a setup. In contrast to the standard setup time, the actual setup time is known only after the completion of the setup.

**Shop Floor Control.** See *Production Activity Control* for definition.

**Shop Floor Resources.** Those resources that the production activity control system uses in managing the transformation of a shop order or job from the time that it is released to the shop floor by the formal planning system to the time that it has been completed or can no longer be processed. Typically, there are four major types of shop floor resources: (1) inventory, (2) tooling, (3) personnel, and (4) machine capacity.

**Shop Load.** See *Load.*

**Shop Loading.** The process of scheduling work into a manufacturing facility. (See *Load.*)

**Shop Order.** Also called a "job," a "manufacturing order," or an "order." The entity that is controlled by the production activity control system as it moves through the various stages on the shop floor. Typically, a shop order is an authorization issued by the planning system to the execution system for the manufacture of a certain quantity of a certain part that is to be available by no later than the due date.

**Shop Packet.** A set of paperwork that travels with the shop order and may include routings, blueprints, material requisitions, move tickets, time tickets, etc. (See *Traveler.*)

**Shorted Order.** A planned order that is currently facing material shortages in one or more of its component items. In general, shorted orders should not be released to the shop floor until the shortages have been relieved. The only exception to this general rule involves the forced release (see *Forced Release*).

**Shortest Operation Time.** See *Shortest Processing Time.*

**Shortest Processing Time.** A dispatching rule that sequences the orders at a work center according to their processing times (setup plus total variable processing time) in that work center. Orders with the shortest processing times have the highest priorities. (See *Dispatching Rule.*)

**SIT.** Shortest imminent processing time. See *Shortest Processing Time.*

**Slack.** The difference in time between the order due date (see *Order Due Date*) and the time at which the order is expected to be completed. Frequently, slack is used as a measure of the degree of urgency associated with an order. It is also used by many due date–based dispatching rules, such as the critical ratio rule and the least slack per remaining operations.

**Slack per Remaining Operations.** A dispatching rule that lets the priority of a job be equal to its slack (Due date − Time now − Remaining processing time) divided by the number of remaining operations. (See *Dispatching Rule; Slack.*)

**SOT.** Shortest operation time. See *Shortest Processing Time.*

**SPT.** See *Shortest Processing Time.*

**Staging.** The physical withdrawal and assembly ("kitting") of component material to ensure its availability. Staging is frequently done before the release of a shop order, at the time that material is checked. The purpose of staging is to identify any material shortages before the order is released.

**Standard Processing Time.** See *Standard Time.*

**Standard Setup Time.** See *Standard Time.*

**Standard Time.** (1) The time that should be needed to set up a given machine or assembly operation (also referred to as "standard setup time"). (2) The time that should be required to run one part/assembly/end product through a given machine or assembly operation (also referred to as "standard processing time") (Fogarty and Hoffmann, 1983, p. 701).

**Stockless Production.** See *Just-in-Time Manufacturing.*

**Tooling.** Equipment and special fixtures such as dies that are used during the setup of a machine or an assembly operation. One of the four major shop resources (the others being labor, machine capacity, and inventory). (See *Tools.*)

**Tooling Requirements.** A determination of the tooling required to complete the setup on a machine or a process.

**Tools.** Items (wrenches, for example) that are used during a setup procedure but are not attached to the machine during setup or considered part of the machine (Hall, 1983, p. 21).

**Transport Time.** The time required to transport parts between two work centers. Transport time can frequently be found in the form of a table (matrix). It is a component of manufacturing lead time (IBM, Glossary, 1972, p. 22), and it can refer to either a standard value (used in the move time standards) or an actual value.

**Traveler.** A copy of the manufacturing order that actually moves with the work through the shop. (See *Shop Packet.*)

**Utilization.** The percentage of time that a machine, work center, line, or facility is *not* down due to equipment failure, lack of material, lack of work, or lack of an operator (Fogarty and Hoffmann, 1983, p. 704).

**Validity.** See *Priority Validity.*

**Vertical Dependency.** A type of dependent priority. Vertical dependency is the realization that the priority of a component order is directly dependent on the availability of an item or items on a higher level in the product structure (Orlicky, 1975, p. 147). (See *Dependent Priority.*)

**Voice Recognition.** A form of automated identification (see *Automated Identification*). Voice recognition is a system by which the employee directly inputs information into the computer by voice.

**Wait Time.** The time that orders spend on the shop floor waiting for transportation. A component of manufacturing lead time. Wait time can refer to either a standard value (i.e., a predetermined time allowance) or an actual value (i.e., the recorded time that the order actually spends waiting for transportation).

**WIP.** See *Work-in-Process*.

**Work Center.** A production facility consisting of one or more people and/or machines that can be viewed as one unit for the purposes of capacity requirements planning and detailed assignment (Fogarty and Hoffmann, 1983, p. 705). (See *Capacity Requirements Planning; Detailed Assignment.*)

**Work-in-Process.** Items in various stages of completion throughout the plant, including raw material that has been released and finished material that is awaiting final inspection or shipment to a customer (Fogarty and Hoffmann, 1983, p. 705). Included in work-in-process inventories are raw material in stock, semifinished component parts in stock, finished component parts in stock, subassemblies in stock, component parts in process, and subassemblies in process (Orlicky, 1975, p. 17).

**Zero Inventory.** See *Just in-Time Manufacturing*.

# Recommended Readings

The following readings are recommended for those interested in learning more about production activity control. Each citation is accompanied by a maximum of four key terms. These key terms identify the major PAC-related topics examined in the article.

Bechte, W. "Controlling Manufacturing Lead Time and Work-in-Process Inventory by means of Load-Oriented Order Release," *American Production and Inventory Control Society 25th Annual Conference Proceedings*. Chicago, 1982, pp. 67–72. (Capacity; Lead time; Order release; Lead time estimation)

Bechtold, R. K. "The Work-Center Syndrome," *American Production and Inventory Control Society 25th Annual Conference Proceedings*. Chicago, 1982, pp. 77–81. (Capacity; Control; Layout)

Belt, B. "Integrating Capacity Planning and Capacity Control." *Production and Inventory Management* 17 (1976), pp. 9–23. (Input/output control; Capacity; Queues; Loading)

Berry, W. L.; T. E. Vollmann; and D. C. Whybark. *Master Production Scheduling: Principles and Practice*. Washington, D. C.: American Production and Inventory Control Society, 1979.

Brooks, R. B. "Shop Dispatching Belongs to the Foreman." *American Production and Inventory Control Society 21st Annual Conference Proceedings*. Hollywood, Fla., 1978, pp. 112–24. (Scheduling (backward); Feedback; Input/output control; Role of the human)

Bruhn, G. L. "Shop Floor Control? You Can't Control if You Don't Know..." *American Production and Inventory Control Society*

*22nd Annual Conference Proceedings.* St. Louis, 1979, pp. 175–76. (Definition; Dispatching; Input/output control; PAC interfaces)

Chamberlain, W. W. "Shop Floor Data Collection—Impact on Top Management." *American Production and Inventory Control Society 25th Annual Conference Proceedings.* Chicago, 1982, pp. 433-35. (Bar coding; Top management; Data collection)

DeWelt, R. L. "Integrating Cost Accounting with Inventory and MRP." *American Production and Inventory Control Society 18th Annual Conference Proceedings.* San Diego, 1975, pp. 275–84. (Accounting; Feedback; Control; Interface to PAC system)

Dyer, W. F. "Shop Orders—The Weak Link in MRP." *American Production and Inventory Control Society 21st Annual Conference Proceedings.* Hollywood, Fla., 1978, pp. 125–32. (MPS; MRP; Requirements of a successful PAC system; Data collection)

———. "Dispatching: A Priority Control Tool." *American Production and Inventory Control Society 22nd Annual Conference Proceedings.* St. Louis, 1979, pp. 182–83. (Dispatching rules; Due dates; Feedback)

Edwards, B., and M. O'Neill. "Checks and Balances in Job Shop Control (or Welcome to the Real World)." *American Production and Inventory Control Society 21st Annual Conference Proceedings.* Hollywood, Fla., 1978, pp. 165–76. (Feedback; Data collection; Implementation)

Ellis, R. B. "Dollarize Your Priority List." *American Production and Inventory Control Society 26th Annual Conference Proceedings.* New Orleans, 1983, pp. 430–32. (Accounting; Dispatching rules; Priorities)

Erickson, J. "Considerations when Implementing Priority Planning." *Production and Inventory Management* 17, no. 3 (1976), pp. 52–60. (MRP; Due dates; Priority planning; Dispatching)

Fogarty, D. W., and T. R. Hoffmann. *Production and Inventory Management.* Cincinnati: South-Western Publishing, 1983, chaps. 12, 14. (MRP; Production activity control; Dispatching; Priorities)

Folse, E. "Work Order Management, Key to Shop Floor Control." *American Production and Inventory Control Society 23rd Annual Conference Proceedings.* Los Angeles, 1980, pp. 362–64. (Order review/release; Control; Feedback)

Foxen, R. W. "Scheduling and Loading." *Production and Inventory Management* 8, no. 3 (1967), pp. 52–68. (Sequencing; Loading; Control; Priorities)

Garwood, D., and J. Civerolo. "A Check List for a Dispatch List." *Production and Inventory Management Review* 1, no. 10 (1981), pp. 24–26. (Production activity control; Dispatching; Priorities; MRP)

Gips, J. "Hidden Hurdles in the Path of Shop Floor Control." *American Production and Inventory Control Society 24th Annual Conference Proceedings.* Boston, 1981, pp. 160–62. (Due dates; Dispatching; PAC requirements)

————. "Good News about Queues." *American Production and Control Society 26th Annual Conference Proceedings.* New Orleans, 1983, pp. 297–99. (Capacity; Input/output control; Priorities; Queues)

Greene, J. H. *Production and Inventory Control: Systems and Decisions.* Homewood, Ill.: Richard D. Irwin, 1974, chaps. 1, 8, 14, 15, 16, 17, 19. (Scheduling; Dispatching; Capacity; Loading)

Grieco, P. L., Jr. "CREP—Capacity Requirements Planning." *American Production and Inventory Control Society 20th Annual Conference Proceedings.* Washington, D.C., 1977, pp. 163–65. (Capacity; Loading; Control; Dispatching)

Griffin, K. R. "Job Shop Scheduling." *Production and Inventory Management* 12, no. 3 (1971), pp. 65–76. (Scheduling; Capacity; Loading; Sequencing)

Groover, M. P. *Automation, Production Systems and Computer Aided Manufacturing.* Englewood Cliffs, N.J.: Prentice Hall, 1980.

Gue, F. S. "Input/Output Control in the Job Shop." *American Production and Inventory Control Society 18th Annual Conference Proceedings.* San Diego, 1975, pp. 58–72. (Input/output control; Capacity; Loading; Expediting)

Hablewitz, M. J., and W. S. Williams. "Integrating Execution and Control of Salvage (Rework) Scheduling on the Shop Floor." *American Production and Inventory Control Society 26th Annual Conference Proceedings.* New Orleans, 1983, pp. 466–69. (Capacity; Scrap; Salvage; Production activity control)

Hall, D. G. "Notes on Integrating Capacity Planning and Capacity Control." *Production and Inventory Management* 17 (1976), pp. 99–115. (Input/output control; Queues; Capacity)

Hall, R. W. *Zero Inventories.* Homewood, Ill.: Dow Jones-Irwin, 1983.

Hanson, S. R. "Integrating Shop Floor Control and Standard Cost Accounting." *American Production and Inventory Control Society 26th Annual Conference Proceedings.* Los Angeles, 1980, pp. 365–68. (Accounting; Feedback; Interfaces; Integration)

Huge, E. C. "Lead Time Management: Your Key to Successful Master Scheduling." *American Production and Inventory Control Society 21st Annual Conference Proceedings.* Hollywood, Fla., 1978, pp. 269–81. (Lead time; Queues)

————. "Managing Manufacturing Lead Times." *Harvard Business Review* 57, no. 5 (September–October 1979), pp. 116–23. (Lead time; Queues)

Hutchings, H. V. "Shop Scheduling and Control." *Production and Inventory Management* 17, no. 1 (1976), pp. 64–93. (Scheduling; Capacity; Priorities; Dispatching)

IBM "Management Overview, System Requirements, Glossary and Index." *Communications Oriented Production Information and Control System,* vol. 1. White Plains, N.Y.: IBM Technical Publications Department, 1972.

IBM. "Chapter 1: Engineering and Production." In *Communications Oriented Production Information and Control System,* vol. 2. White Plains, N.Y.: IBM Technical Publications Department, 1972. (Engineering; Maintenance, Preventive; Maintenance, scheduling)

————. "Chapter 6: Manufacturing Activity Planning." In *Communications Oriented Production Information and Control System,* vol. 5. White Plains, N.Y.: IBM Technical Publications Department, 1972. (Queues; Sequencing; Loading; Dispatching)

————."Chapter 7: Order Release." In *Communications Oriented Production Information and Control System,* vol. 5. White Plains, N.Y.: IBM Technical Publications Department, 1972. (Order review/release)

————. "Chapter 8: Plant Monitoring and Control." *Communications Oriented Production Information and Control System,* vol. 6. White Plains, N.Y.: IBM Technical Publications Department, 1972. (Scheduling; Data collection/monitoring; Control/feedback; Tooling)

————. "Chapter 9: Plant Maintenance." In *Communications Oriented Production Information and Control System,* vol. 6. White Plains, N.Y.: IBM Technical Publications Department, 1972. (Maintenance, preventive; Maintenance, scheduling)

Kanet, J. J. "On the Advisability of Operation Due Dates." *American Production and Inventory Control Society 23rd Annual Conference Proceedings.* Los Angeles, 1980, pp. 355–57. (Due dates; Dispatching rules; Sequencing)

————. "A Critical Look at the Critical Ratio." *American Production and Inventory Control Society 24th Annual Conference Proceed-*

*ings.* Boston, 1981, pp. 182–84. (Priorities; Sequencing; Dispatching Rules)

Lankford, R. L. "Short Term Planning of Manufacturing Capacity." *American Production and Inventory Control Society 21st Annual Conference Proceedings.* Hollywood, Fla., 1978, pp. 37–68. (CRP; Lead time; Queues; Input/output control)

———. "Input/Output Control: Making It Work." *American Production and Inventory Control Society 23rd Annual Conference Proceedings.* Los Angeles, 1980, pp. 419–20. (Lead time; Input/output control)

Levulis, R. J. "Group Technology Strategies in the U.S.A." *Spring Annual Conference Proceedings—AIIE, Atlanta,* 1980, pp. 267–73.

Mather, H., and G. Plossl. "Priority Fixation vs. Throughput Planning." *Production and Inventory Management* 18, no. 3 (1977), pp. 27–51. (Priorities; Capacity; Lead time)

May, N. P. "Queue Control: Utopia or Pie in the Sky?" *American Production and Inventory Control Society 23rd Annual Conference Proceedings.* Los Angeles, 1980, pp. 358–61. (Queues; Capacity; Control; Feedback)

———. "Shop Floor Control—Principles and Uses." *American Production and Inventory Control Society 24th Annual Conference Proceedings.* Boston, 1981, pp. 170–74. (Dispatching rules; Sequencing; Order review/release; Production activity control interfaces)

McEneny, T. "Shop Floor Control: The Five Keys to Success." *American Production and Inventory Control Society 25th Annual Conference Proceedings.* Chicago, 1982, pp. 94–96. (Production activity control; Capacity; Master production schedule; Work-in-process)

Meck, R. A., Jr. "Maximizing the Full Benefits of Shop Floor Control." *American Production and Inventory Control Society 18th Annual Conference Proceedings.* San Diego, 1975, pp. 80–84. (Production activity control; Feedback; Data collection; Tracking)

Melnyk, S. A.; P. L. Carter; D. M. Dilts; and D. M. Lyth. *Shop Floor Control.* Homewood, Ill.: Dow Jones-Irwin, 1985. (Production activity control; Capacity; Principles; Dispatching rules)

Milwaukee APICS Chapter. *Shop Floor Control.* Training aid published by APICS, 1972. (Production activity control; Dispatching; Loading; Feedback)

Nellemann, D. O. "Closing the Shop Floor Control Financial Loop." *American Production and Inventory Control Society 23rd Annual*

*Conference Proceedings.* Los Angeles, 1980, pp. 308–12. (Finance; Accounting; Feedback; Integration)

New, C. C. "Job Shop Scheduling: Who Needs a Computer to Sequence Jobs?" *Production and Inventory Management* 16, no. 4 (1975), pp. 38–45. (Priorities; Sequencing; Dispatching rules)

Nordskog, W. H. "Queue Control: A Case Study." *American Production and Inventory Control Society 19th Annual Conference Proceedings.* Atlanta, 1976, pp. 327–32. (Queues; Maintenance; Loading; Lead time)

Orlicky, J. A. *Materials Requirements Planning.* New York: McGraw-Hill, 1975.

Perreault, A. "The Bottom Line of Shop Floor Control Begins with a Good Data Collection System." *American Production and Inventory Control Society 21st Annual Conference Proceedings.* Hollywood, Fla., 1978, pp. 103–11. (Tracking; Priorities; Feedback; Accounting)

Plossl, G. W., and O. W. Wight. *Production and Inventory Control.* Englewood Cliffs, N.J.: Prentice-Hall, 1967. Chaps. 8, 9, 10, 11. (Dispatching; MRP; Loading; Inventory)

Prather, K. L. "Seven Deadly Sins of Production Control." *American Production and Inventory Control Society 26th Annual Conference Proceedings.* New Orleans, 1983, pp. 218–20. (Capacity; Expediting; Lead time; Priorities)

Raffish, N. "Let's Help Shop Floor Control." *Production and Inventory Management Review* 1, no. 7 (July 1981), pp. 17–19. (Productivity; Production activity control; Data collection)

Schonberger, R. J. "Clearest-Road-Ahead Priorities for Shop Floor Control: Moderating Infinite-Capacity-Loading Unevenness." *Production and Inventory Management* 20, no. 2 (1979), pp. 17–29. (Priorities; Capacity; Dispatching)

Sherrill, R. C. "Development of Shop Floor Control." *American Production and Inventory Control Society 19th Annual Conference Proceedings.* Atlanta, 1976, pp. 127–31. (Loading; Data collection; Tracking)

———. "Hot Lists to Queue List." *American Production and Inventory Control Society 20th Annual Conference Proceedings.* Washington, D.C., 1977, pp. 428–33. (Dispatching; Feedback; Control)

Swem, N. C. "From 'Aw Shucks' to 'Attaboy'—Shop Floor Control." *American Production and Inventory Control Society 21st Annual Conference Proceedings.* Hollywood, Fla., 1978, pp. 148–64. (Priorities; Revisions)

Van DeMark, R. L. "Adjust Your Capacity, Do Not Reschedule Your Shop Order." *American Production and Inventory Control Society 24th Annual Conference Proceedings.* Boston, 1981, pp. 148–51. (Capacity; Loading; Priorities; Scheduling)

Vollmann, T. E.; W. L. Berry; and D. Clay Whybark. *Manufacturing Planning and Control Systems.* Homewood, Ill.: Dow Jones-Irwin, 1984, chaps. 4, 5, 13. (Capacity; Priorities; data Collection)

Wallace, T. F. *APICS Dictionary.* 4th ed. Washington, D.C.: American Production and Inventory Control Society, 1980.

Wassweiler, W. R. "Shop Floor Control." *American Production and Inventory Control Society 20th Annual Conference Proceedings.* Washington, D.C., 1977, pp. 386–94. (Dispatching rules; Feedback; Human in the system; Interfaces)

―――――. "The Impact of MRP on Shop Floor Control." *American Production and Inventory Control Society 22nd Annual Conference Proceedings.* St. Louis, 1979, p. 190. (MRP; Order review/release)

―――――. "Fundamentals of Shop Floor Control." *American Production and Inventory Control Society 23rd Annual Conference Proceedings.* Los Angeles, 1980, pp. 352–54. (MRP; Data base; Dispatching; Control)

―――――. "Tool Requirements Planning." *American Production and Inventory Control Society 25th Annual Conference Proceedings.* Chicago, 1982, pp. 160–62. (Routing; Tooling)

Wight, O. W. "Input/Output Control: A Real Handle on Lead Time." *Production and Inventory Management* 11, no. 3 (1970), pp. 9–30. (Input/output control; Capacity; Lead time)

Wolfmeyer, K. "Lead Time in the Job Shop." *Production and Inventory Management* 21, no. 1 (1980), pp. 87–96. (Lead time; Input/output control)

Young, J. B. "Manufacturing Activity Planning—MAP to Success." *American Production and Inventory Control Society 21st Annual Conference Proceedings.* Hollywood, Fla., 1978, pp. 18–25. (Order review/release; Dispatching; Capacity)

―――――. "Understanding Shop Lead Times." *American Production and Inventory Control Society 22nd Annual Conference Proceedings.* St. Louis, 1979, pp. 177–79. (Lead time; Queues; MRP)

―――――. "Practical Dispatching." *American Production and Inventory Control Society 24th Annual Conference Proceedings.* Boston, 1981, pp. 175–77. (Dispatching; Dispatching rules; Priorities)

# INDEX